PAGODA Books

3A
Third Edition

SLE

SPEAKING · LISTENING · EXPRESSION

SLE 3A Third Edition

Copyright © 2008 PAGODA Academy, Inc.

Published by Wit & Wisdom
Wit & Wisdom is the professional language publishing company of the
PAGODA Education Group.
19F, PAGODA Tower, 419, Gangnam-daero,
Seocho-gu, Seoul, 06614, Rep. of KOREA
www.pagodabook.com

Imprint | PAGODA Books

First published 2008
Eleventh impression 2020
Printed in the Republic of Korea

ISBN 978-89-6281-387-6 (13740)

Publisher	Ru-Da Go
Writer	Pagoda Language Education Center
Editors	Robert Vernon, Miran Syn
Advisor	Ruda Go
Illustrator	Ki-Soo Kwon

A defective book may be exchanged at the store where you purchased it.

To Our Students

You hold in your hands a book that has been nearly 20 years in the making. Since 1985, Pagoda Academy has been developing its SLE program to be one of the most popular and effective conversational English programs in Korea. Since the beginning, the experience and observations of the Pagoda instructors have gone into all of the material designed for the SLE courses. With each successive version of the textbooks, the writers have tried to build on the strengths of previous versions, while reflecting changes in teaching methodology and input from both instructors and students. This book is no exception.

For the current version of the SLE 3 textbooks, we have assumed that students should have already acquired a reasonably good foundation of practical knowledge regarding the most common aspects of English. Thus, as opposed to lower levels of the program that focus primarily on building familiarity with indispensable functions and structures, Level 3 focuses almost exclusively on expression - helping you to go beyond mere knowledge of the mechanics of English to naturally develop a fluent command of conversational English. This is done by providing you with stimulating material and engaging activities to encourage you to practice expressing yourself on a wide variety of topics.

However, no book can promise to deliver noticeable improvement in your English ability. The reason is that in order to make improvements to your English fluency, you must practice speaking as much as possible, and no conversational English textbook can make you speak. We have done our best to produce a book full of interesting topics and activities that will get even the most reserved among you talking. However, a book, no matter how well-written, is still just a book. Only you can improve your English fluency. And to do that you must overcome your shyness, frustration, pride and fear of making mistakes, and make an effort to speak. This will challenge you to believe in yourself and to take the Pagoda motto to heart:

"I Can Do It."

Book Format for Level 3A

Overall Format

Each of the twenty lessons in this textbook focuses on a different topic, all of which have been chosen because they are of interest to a wide range of English students. The topics provide a focal point for each lesson, such that all of the vocabulary, reading passages, dialogues, conversation activities and discussion questions examine different aspects of the topic. Each lesson contains enough material to constitute approximately two hours of class time, and includes the following elements.

Lesson Format

Language Points

Each lesson is introduced by a list of vocabulary items that have been chosen because they are useful for discussing the topic of the lesson. Although some or even all of these items may be familiar to you already, the reason for including them is not merely to check that you can recognize them, but to encourage you to practice using them. Try to create opportunities in class to use the items in this section.

Dialogue

Almost every lesson includes a dialogue. This conversation, which uses some of the expressions from the Language Points section, focuses on the topic of the lesson in some way. It also raises relevant issues that your instructor may choose to discuss. Recordings of the dialogues are available for use in class or for self-study.

Reading

In nearly every lesson, there are reading passages that relate to the topic of the lesson. They also deal with interesting aspects of the topics that you instructor may choose to discuss with you in class. Although the reading passages have been produced specifically for this textbook, an effort has made to write material that you would typically find in a variety of different real-life contexts. Recordings of the readings are also available.

Conversation Activities

Each lesson contains at least two conversation activities, designed to give you the opportunity to explore the topic of the lesson in different ways with your classmates and teacher.

Discussion Questions

At the end of each lesson, there is a list of questions dealing with many different sides of the topic. These have been designed to encourage you to express your opinions, share your experiences with the class, and spark conversation.

Goals for the Course

1. You should be more comfortable discussing:

a. The English education system and your experiences at school and university
b. Public morals and ethics, and the loss of a basic sense of right and wrong
c. Your feelings and emotions
d. Job interviews and career options
e. Relationships between men and women, and finding the right partner
f. Socializing and friendship
g. Money management
h. The future and your future plans

2. You should be better able to perform the following functions:

a. Make suggestions, and ask for and receive advice
b. Analyze moral dilemmas and negotiate solutions with classmates
c. Give effective answers to interview questions
d. Describe friends and friendships
e. Make predictions about the future and express your future aspirations and plans

3. You should be better able to use the following grammatical structures:

a. The present perfect
b. Comparatives and superlatives
c. Conditional clauses
d. The future tense

3A

Table of Contents

1 English Education

Language Points

more than a little

My friend studied English in London for almost five years. Her parents spent more than a little money to help her develop her language skills.

to spend a fortune on something

He takes three private lessons a week. He must be spending a fortune on his private tutor!

to have a good shot at doing something

Last year, she achieved a TOEIC score of 880. She's been studying hard, so she has a good shot at achieving her goal of 900 this year.

to stop at nothing

His parents will stop at nothing to make sure that he speaks English well. They send him to many language schools, have hired a private tutor, and plan to send him abroad to study English.

to give someone an edge / the upper hand

Can you believe she got a score of 980 on her TOEIC test? That really gives her the upper hand in her search for a job.

rat race

Spending so much time working, studying English, and worrying about language test scores has created a difficult daily routine for many Korean adults. It is a bit of a rat race.

Reading

South Korean students are **more than a little** obsessed with learning English. Koreans **spend a fortune on** everything from books, CDs, CD-ROMs, online lectures and other Internet content to English language institutes, private tutors, and trips abroad in order **to give themselves the best shot at** learning to speak English fluently. Many statistics and facts from the year 2007 reveal the extent to which learning English has become the focus of a lot of the time, money and effort that Koreans invest in their future. Consider the following:

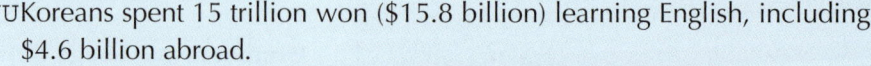

ƒÜKoreans spent 15 trillion won ($15.8 billion) learning English, including $4.6 billion abroad.

ƒÜKorea spent more money per capita on English education than any other country.

ƒÜ102,340 of 554,942 TOEFL applicants worldwide were Korean.

ƒÜAbout 500 Koreans traveled abroad every month to take the TOEFL test because demand to take the test far outstrips the supply of places available at TOEFL test centers in Korea.

ƒÜKoreans spent 700 billion won on English examination fees.

ƒÜ250,000 Koreans under age 29 studied abroad, including 93,000 who went for language study.

ƒ℧There were an estimated 200,000 stay-behind fathers, or "goose fathers," who lived alone in Korea after their wives and children had gone abroad to study English.

Many Koreans **will stop at nothing** to learn English because speaking it fluently has become critical to professional success. High English proficiency test scores and a good command of English **give candidates the upper hand** in the **ruthless** competition for secure, well-paid jobs. And once you have a job, fluency can put your career on the fast track, while a poor command may hold back career advancement. As businesses become increasingly involved in international trade, being able to speak English fluently **gives you a distinct edge** in the **rat race**, and has become one way to gain social status.

Comprehension

1. Can you summarize the reading passage in your own words?

2. Do any of the statistics listed in the first paragraph surprise you? Why?

3. What reason(s) are given for Koreans' obsession with English?

4. Do you think that the observations on the role of English in Korea are accurate? What would you add or change?

Activity A

Preferences and Expectations

With your classmate(s), take turns completing the following sentences. Ask each other questions to get more details.

1 The reason I am learning English is...

2 I have been studying English for...

3 In previous conversation classes, I have been most satisfied with...

4 In previous conversation classes, I have been most dissatisfied with...

5 I think the perfect English conversation teacher should...

6 I think an English conversation teacher shouldn't...

7 I think that an ideal English student should...

8 The thing I find the most challenging about learning English is...

9 The thing I enjoy most about learning English is...

10 In this class, I expect to... I am taking this class because...

11 An excellent strategy for learning English is...

12 To improve my english, I need to...

An English conversation instructor talks to one of her students after class.

Jenny: What did you want to see me about, Kang?

Kang: Well, I've been really frustrated with how slowly my English is improving. I can't seem to make any progress at all. I keep making the same mistakes over and over, and I always forget all of the new vocabulary that I try to learn. What can I do?

Jenny: Learning English takes a long time, you know? You've got to stick with it. You are improving, even if you don't feel like you are. What sort of things are you doing outside of class to study English?

Kang: Nothing, really. My schedule is so **hectic** these days. So I don't have enough time to study English.

Jenny: **I don't believe that for a second**. Don't you read the newspaper?

Kang: Sure. Every day.

Jenny: A Korean newspaper, or an English one?

Kang: Well, Korean, of course. I couldn't read an English newspaper!

Jenny: Sure, you could. It might take you a little longer, and you might have to look up a few words in the dictionary, but if you try, you might be amazed how much you can understand. Your English is actually quite good.

Kang: Thanks, but I don't think…

Jenny: You know, reading the newspaper is a pretty natural way to improve your vocabulary, your reading comprehension, and the variety of English sentence structures you use. And it's certainly more interesting than reading vocabulary builders or grammar textbooks.

Kang: I guess so.

Jenny: Give it a try, and let me know how you **make out**. I'd better get to my next class. See you tomorrow.

Kang: Okay, thanks.

Definitely...not!

For each of the following statements, indicate how strongly you agree or disagree. Then discuss your reasons with your classmate(s) what your reasons are.

① Disagree Strongly	② Disagree Somewhat	③ Indifferent	④ Agree Somewhat	⑤ Agree Strongly

❶ Learning English should be fun.		① ② ③ ④ ⑤
❷ Learning English should be a lot of work.		① ② ③ ④ ⑤
❸ Studying lists of vocabulary helps me improve my English.		① ② ③ ④ ⑤
❹ Watching English movies or television (American sitcoms, BBC, CNN, etc.) is useful.		① ② ③ ④ ⑤
❺ Reading English newspapers or magazines is useful.		① ② ③ ④ ⑤
❻ English conversation teachers should correct all mistakes.		① ② ③ ④ ⑤
❼ English conversation teachers should talk very little.		① ② ③ ④ ⑤
❽ Speaking to other students is useless.		① ② ③ ④ ⑤
❾ Studying English grammar is boring, but important.		① ② ③ ④ ⑤
❿ The more I study, the faster my English improves.		① ② ③ ④ ⑤
⓫ Learning English is a lifelong process.		① ② ③ ④ ⑤
⓬ I only need to learn American English.		① ② ③ ④ ⑤
⓭ Listening to other people talk is the best way to learn English.		① ② ③ ④ ⑤
⓮ Studying with a private tutor is the only way to improve quickly.		① ② ③ ④ ⑤
⓯ The older you are, the harder it is to learn English.		① ② ③ ④ ⑤
⓰ Learning how to write in English (emails, text messages, essays, etc.) is important.		① ② ③ ④ ⑤
⓱ Fluency is more important than accuracy.		① ② ③ ④ ⑤
⓲ Korean high school and university students can benefit a lot from studying in an English-speaking country.		① ② ③ ④ ⑤
⓳ It's very important to have good pronunciation.		① ② ③ ④ ⑤
⓴ I try to pronounce English as closely as possible to the way native speakers do.		① ② ③ ④ ⑤
㉑ I don't worry about making mistakes in English class.		① ② ③ ④ ⑤
㉒ I often practice my English outside of class.		① ② ③ ④ ⑤
㉓ I try to "think in English" as much as I can; I try not to translate from Korean when I am speaking.		① ② ③ ④ ⑤

Revise Korea's English Education System

You and your partner(s) work for the Ministry of Education. Your ministry hired educational consultants to study the Korean English education system. Their 10 recommendations are presented below. You and your partner(s) must decide which (if any) recommendations to implement. Classify each recommendation as follows:

A: This is a good recommendation, and it can be implemented quickly.

B: This is a good recommendation, but it can be implemented only in the long-term.

C: This recommendation could be good, but it needs to be revised.

D: This is a poor recommendation. Implementing it would be foolish.

The Consultants' 10 Recommendations to Improve the Korean English Education System

1. Reading and grammar are emphasized too much in public schools. The curriculum should be redesigned to stress spoken skills and listening comprehension.

2. Some subjects other than English (math, geography, etc.) should be taught in English. Either some Korean teachers should receive English language training so that they are able to teach their subject in English, or foreigners should be hired to teach these subjects in English.

3. Private language institutes should be allowed to offer English classes 24 hours a day.

4. All Korean teachers of English must have either a master's degree in English or extensive experience living in an English-speaking country.

5. The government should launch many more programs to train teachers effectively in English and teaching methodology.

6. To encourage more talented students to pursue a career teaching English, salaries for Korean English teachers should be substantially increased.

7. The government should give tax incentives to encourage the creation of TV and radio stations that promote the use of English.

8. The government should assist middle and high schools to create foreign exchange programs. (e.g., the government could create an agency to recruit native English-speaking students to live in Korean homes, and support Korean students to make the return trip to an English-speaking country.)

9. Standardized testing of English should begin in elementary school. To graduate from high school, students should be required to pass a standardized spoken English exam.

10. From students' first English class in elementary school, English should be taught in English only. Teachers should use Korean only to explain grammar.

Your Own Recommendations to Improve Korea's English Education System

What additional changes to Korea's English education system would you suggest? Consider the following areas:

- Public schools
- Foreign teachers' qualifications
- Cultural exchange programs
- Examination systems

- Private language institutes
- Tax incentives
- Radio and TV stations
- Domestic teachers' salaries and qualifications

Be prepared to explain to the class which of the consultants' recommendations you agree with (and why), as well as your own recommendations. Be prepared to present your ideas for a new Korean English education system to the class!

Discussion

1. Do you sometimes resent having to study English? Explain why.

2. Besides getting a good job, what other reasons do you have for studying English?

3. What is the highest amount you would be willing to pay an English tutor for an hour of teaching?

4. When you speak English, do you try to imitate the accent of a British or American person? Do you feel that sounding like a British or American person means giving up your identity?

5. Are you confident speaking English in front of native speakers? Are you confident speaking English in front of Koreans?

6. What kinds of negative and positive effects does learning English have on children?

7. Do you think that most children like or dislike learning English? Why?

8. When and if you have a child, what will your plan be regarding his/her English education? Do you believe in English language early-childhood education? What won't you do?

9. What are some of the best ways you've heard of to improve a child's ability to speak English?

10. A growing number of Korean children live abroad with their mothers to learn English. Do you think that this is a good thing? What are the pros and cons for the children? For mothers and fathers? For families? For Korea?

11. Would you support a decision to make English the official second language of Korea? What effects do you think this would have?

12. Do you think that English education is too highly valued in Korea?

13. Describe some of the factors that make English so difficult to learn.

14. Is it possible for a Korean to learn to speak English like a native speaker without overseas study?

15. What are some of the characteristics of a good language learner?

16. Do you think that English conversation teachers should correct important mistakes while you are speaking? Or do you think that English conversation teachers should write down important mistakes you make, and correct them after you have spoken?

17. What are some really good methods that you use for improving your spoken English? What methods would you recommend to your partner(s)?

2 Be True to Your School

LESSON

Language Points

alma mater
> I am so proud of my alma mater. I often return for reunions, and sometimes I donate money to the university.

fraternity/sorority
> My friend is a university student in the US. She has joined a sorority and spends a lot of her time with her sorority sisters.

to get your foot in the door
> Sometimes, an old university friend can help you get your foot in the door at a company where he works.

connections / to make connections / to use your connections / through connections
> For some university students, making connections is more important than gaining knowledge.

to network
> Networking with your classmates in business school can help you become successful in business in the future.

alumni / alumnus / alumna
> I had never met him before, but when I learned that he was an alumnus of the university I attended, I felt an instant bond with him.

to pull an all-nighter
> That was such a long project to complete! I had to pull an all-nighter to finish it.

to cram (for exams)
> Exams are next week. I'm still unprepared. I have to start cramming.

Reading

When it comes to friendship and social activities, relationships based on what schools one has attended are generally unimportant in English-speaking countries. However, the situation is very different is some parts of the world. This is especially true in Asia, where class reunions and school ties often play an important part in young people's lives, and relationships forged at school extend well into adulthood.

Many people from English-speaking countries are likely to be proud of their **alma mater**. However, unlike in Asia, they don't necessarily feel an especially close bond with strangers just because those people happen to have attended the same university, high school, etc. When students in English-speaking countries form close friendships with people they meet at university, it is usually with people who had the same interests, who belonged to the same clubs, played on the same sports team, etc. In the US, there are also special university social clubs called **fraternities** for men and **sororities** for women. Though not as popular as they once were, they still exist in colleges and universities across America and attract new members every year. Approximately 13 percent of male students and 11 percent of female students belong to a social fraternity or sorority.

These differences aside, in both Asian and English-speaking societies, school ties can be helpful in getting a job. Knowing a person who already works at a company can help you **get your foot in the door**. In English, we call them "**connections**." Forming and maintaining such relationships is called "**networking**." Universities can be very good places **to network**. If a Human Resources manager is looking over your application, he/she may be more likely to invite you for an interview if you have attended the same university he/she did.

Comprehension

1. Summarize the article in your own words.

2. In what way does the author say the attitudes of students in English-speaking countries toward school relationships differ from those in Asia?

3. What does "networking" mean?

4. Do you agree with what the author says about the role played by alumni relationships? Why or why not?

Activity A

What university did for me...

Getting into university requires hard work, and attending university requires a lot of money. But how does a university education really help you? For each number, decide which statement (A or B) is more true for you. In some cases, both statements (A and B) or neither statement might be true for you. Discuss the statements with your classmate(s) and talk about your university experience. Ask each other follow-up questions to find out more information.

In university...

A	B
❶ I have joined/joined groups and clubs and learned about team spirit.	❶ I have partied/partied as much as possible.
❷ I have become/became more informed about social problems and political issues.	❷ I have become/became cynical.
❸ I have learned/learned how to socialize and feel comfortable in front of others.	❸ I have sometimes got/sometimes got so drunk that I did things I wish I couldn't remember.
❹ I have learned/learned how to interact with the opposite sex.	❹ I have had/had many boyfriends/girlfriends in university.

⑤ I have learned / learned self-discipline and responsibility.

⑥ I have acquired / acquired knowledge which is useful in my everyday life.

⑦ I have gained / gained specialized skills and knowledge which I (will) find useful in my career.

⑧ I have learned / learned how to reason and argue my point effectively

⑨ I have made / made important **connections** which (will be) have been important in advancing my career.

⑩ I have made / made friendships, some of which (will last) have lasted after graduation.

⑤ I have pulled / **pulled all-nighters** and **crammed for exams**.

⑥ I have learned / learned how to make witty conversation to impress the opposite sex.

⑦ Nothing I have learned / learned in university is useful, but my degree (will look) looks nice.

⑧ I have learned / learned to BS my way through any situation.

⑨ I have kissed up / kissed up to the right people, and I know who to call on when I need a favor.

⑩ I will get together / get together with other **alumni** and get just as drunk as we used to.

Activity B

Where Are They Now?

Think about your experience in: elementary school, middle school, high school, and university. With your classmates, discuss the people and memories described below. Ask each other follow-up questions to get more information.

- The person you hated most
- The person you envied most
- The person you secretly had a crush on
- The person you wish you had never broken up with

- The person you miss the most
- The biggest bully
- The strangest person
- The person you thought was most likely to succeed
- The person you would most like to see again
- The funniest person
- Your happiest memory
- Your proudest moment
- The most interesting club / team you belonged to
- Your happiest learning experience
- A time when you skipped something important
- A time when you embarrassed yourself
- A memorable trip you took with classmates

Your Most Memorable Teachers

Think about your experience in: elementary school, middle school, high school, and university. With your classmates, discuss the teachers/professors below. Ask each other follow-up questions to get more information

- The best teacher you had
- The best English teacher you had
- Your most inspirational teacher
- The teacher who always seemed to be in a bad mood
- The teacher who made learning fun

- Your funniest teacher
- The teacher you learned the most from
- The teacher you adored the most
- The teacher you despised the most

Your Favorite Teacher

Tell your partner(s) about your favorite teacher at school. Look at the list below, and choose the topics that you want to talk about.

- What was his/her name?
- Was he/she strict or lenient?
- What subject did he/she teach?
- How would you describe his/her teaching style?
- Were you good at the subject?
- What activities did you do in class?
- What was special about him/her?

- What made him/her different from your other teachers?
- Did you work hard and a learn lot in his/her class?
- Was he/she also the favorite teacher of many other students? Why?
- When were you last in touch with him/her?

Discussion

1. Have you ever been to a class reunion? Did you enjoy the experience? Were the people you went to school with very different when you met them again? Did they think that you had changed? If so, how?

2. What is the main reason you would be interested in attending a school reunion? To measure your success against that of your peers? To see what your old classmates have been up to? Or for some other reason?

3. Tell you classmates about your closest friends in elementary, middle, and high school. When did you meet? Why did you become such good friends? Do you still keep in touch with them? Do you still see them? If not, would you like to see them again? Why or why not? How do you think you would act if you met them again?

4. How important are school ties in your life? Do many of your former schools' alumni play important roles in your life? If so, how?

5. Do you feel a special bond with people who have gone to the same schools that you have? Why or why not? Do you ever resent or try to avoid the social obligations that come with being an alumnus of a certain school?

6. Do you still keep in touch with any of the friends you made in middle school, highschool or university? How often?

7. In your opinion and experience, how important are **connections** and **networking** in getting a job?

8. If you have graduated from university, do you feel a strong attachment and commitment to your **alma mater**?

3 Morally Bankrupt

Language Points

behind (someone's) back

I can't believe that he has been spreading rumors about me behind my back! We can't be friends anymore.

be ashamed of (someone)

You've been cheating on your girlfriend? You should be ashamed of yourself!

to feel guilt / to feel guilty / to feel remorse / to be remorseful

He felt guilty about committing the crime. He appeared remorseful in front of the judge, so he got only a small fine and a warning.

peer pressure / to give in to peer pressure

Many teenagers give in to peer pressure. When they are with their friends, they do things that they know are wrong.

to evade taxes / evading taxes / tax evasion

Al Capone never spent time in jail for murder, but served more than seven years for tax evasion.

to set an example for (someone) / to set an example of (someone)

My parents always set a good example for me. I have never seen them do anything unethical.

to falsify

The company had been falsifying its financial records for years. So when the company finally went bankrupt and investors lost their money, many accountants went to jail.

impartial

I hate judged competitions because the judges are rarely impartial.

Dialogue

Two young men talking at a night club.

Robert: ...So, anyways, that's the reason I think we never got the contract.

Michael: Ah... Hey, do you want to stay here or **head** somewhere else?

Robert: I was just about to order another round, but okay. **I'm up for** almost anything. Why? You don't like it here?

Michael: I just want to get out of here. I was **hitting on this chick** on the way back from the bathroom, but her boyfriend **spotted** us. So, why don't we **hit the road**?

Robert: Are you serious? But, you're a married man! What the heck were you thinking?

Michael: Oh, come on, man; don't give me that **holier-than-thou** stuff. You're not telling me that you've never had a little fun on the side **behind your**

wife's back. Why don't we go to Holyfield's? It's a **younger crowd** there, and the **chicks** are **hotter**.

Robert: Don't you feel guilty? How can you face your wife?

Michael: She'll never find out. She thinks I'm working late at the office. And, you know, who cares?

Robert: That's so...**sleazy**. How would you feel if she did the same thing to you? You should **be ashamed of yourself**.

Michael: Come on, everyone does it.

Robert: No, man. Not everyone. Listen, here's some money to cover my share of the tab. I think I'm going to **head home**. I thought we were just going out after work for a couple of drinks, but it sounds like you've got other plans. I'll see you around the office.

Michael: But it's only 11 o'clock.

Robert: Yeah, I know. My wife's **waiting up for** me.

Comprehension

1. Briefly summarize what happened at the bar. Why does Michael want to leave?

2. What is Robert's opinion of his co-worker?

3. Why do you think Robert wants to go home early?

4. What would you have done in Robert's position?

Activity A

Not Like They Used To Be

Many things have changed in the last 30 years. Many people think that some of those changes have been for the worse. Choose a few of the categories below and tell your partner(s) what you think. For each category that you have chosen, answer:

- In what ways have things changed?
- Have things become worse, become better, or stayed the same?
- What are some examples to support your opinions?
- Do these changes reflect a widespread loss of basic morality?

Style of dress and hairstyles	Respect for teachers
Family values	Work ethic
Respect for traditional authority figures	Attitudes toward neighbors
Attitudes towards extramarital sex	Generosity towards the needy
Respect for authority	Attitudes towards premarital sex
Attitudes towards the law	Social conscience and activism
Attitudes towards child-rearing	Trust in the government

Reading

Are we losing our morals? It's not uncommon to hear stories in the media about the good deeds of common citizens. It is also reported that more people than ever are volunteering their time to help the poor, the sick, and the elderly. Nonetheless, there is also a lot of evidence of a widespread lack of basic morality.

Immoral behaviour can be found in all areas of society. Most high school students experience a lot of peer pressure to do things they consider to be wrong, and it is only the most self-confident or unpopular who can risk not **complying**. In many high schools in the West, high school students are experimenting with smoking, drinking, drugs and sex. Violent behaviour, and mistreating or excluding unpopular students has become routine.

Parents, who are supposed to act as role models and **set a good example for** their children, are just as likely to break generally accepted codes of behaviour. For instance, they routinely break traffic rules just to save a couple of minutes.

Office workers are guilty of unethical behaviour on a daily basis - misusing their expense accounts, stealing company property, lying about what they did or did not do, using sick days inappropriately, and the list goes on. Usually they excuse their behaviour by saying things like, "If I didn't do it, someone else would" or "It's okay...everyone does it."

Even at the highest levels of business, executives admit they are willing **to falsify** their accounting records to gain an advantage over their competitors. A surprising 75% of MBA students say they would be willing to change the facts to make company profits look good. This lack of moral self-control is common in the workplace.

We frequently face temptations to do what we know is wrong and many of us could improve our day-to-day behaviour in some ways. Of course, we can't all be like Mother Teresa, but if you don't change your behaviour, who will?

Comprehension

1. Can you summarize this article in your own words?

2. Give some examples of temptations that high school students, adults, and office workers face.

3. Do you agree with the above article? Do you think that the author's views are accurate? Or do you think they are idealistic? In your opinion, is the author realistic or pessimistic about human nature?

Activity B

Moral Dilemmas

Discuss the following moral dilemmas with your group. Consider each situation carefully and discuss what you would do in such situations.

Callous Jogger

You are out running one day along your usual route when you see someone drowning in a river. The person obviously cannot swim, and probably won't last more than a couple of minutes against the strong current. No one else is around. Would you risk drowning to save a stranger? Are you morally or legally **obligated** to do so?

The Overcrowded Lifeboat

The year is 1840, and you are the captain of a ship that has struck an iceberg and sunk in the middle of the Atlantic. You and 30 other passengers are crammed into a tiny life-raft intended to carry only 8. The raft is taking on water fast and you are forced to make a decision: To save some of the passengers, you must throw some passengers overboard; otherwise, the raft will sink and you will all drown. Which would you choose? If you chose to throw some people out, how would you decide who it would be?

Pangs of Conscience

You have an important job and many people depend on you. If you ever lost your job, many people would be inconvenienced. Nonetheless, you have been **pilfering** supplies from the company for your son to use at school for several months now. The boss has **caught on** and goes hunting for the **culprit**. He narrows down the suspects to one: a cleaning lady. He confronts her and, although she protests, he fires her on the spot. Would you confess or keep quiet?

The Partiality of Friendship

You are in charge of hiring someone to fill a position at your company. Your friend has applied and is qualified, but someone else seems even more qualified. You want to give the job to your friend, but you feel guilty, believing that you ought to be **impartial**. But on the other hand, doesn't friendship have a moral importance that permits, and perhaps even requires, partiality in some situations? Who would you hire?

Word of Honor

A friend **confides in** you that he has committed a particular crime and you promise never to tell anyone. Discovering that an innocent person has been accused of the crime, you **plead with** your friend to give himself up. He refuses and reminds you of your promise. What should you do? In general, under what conditions should promises be broken?

Lets Put the Hurt On Him

A terrorist who has threatened to explode several bombs in crowded areas has been **apprehended**. Unfortunately, he has already **planted** the bombs and they are scheduled to go off in a short time. It is possible that hundreds of people may die. If you were the **interrogator**, would you **resort to** torture to make him talk? Why or why not?

Doctor's Dilemma

You are a psychiatrist and your patient has just told you that he intends to kill a particular woman. You can't be sure if he is serious or not. Should you report the threat to the police and the woman or should you remain silent as the principle of **confidentiality** between doctor and patient demands? Should there be a law that **compels** you to report such threats?

Activity C

You Must Be Joking!

Work with your classmate(s). Look at the following statements and say whether you agree or disagree. Support your opinion, giving examples where necessary.

Charity starts at home. Why should I donate my money or time to others when I need to work hard just to support my own family?

If no one gets hurt, it is perfectly acceptable to break traffic laws.

Who has the right to tell teenagers not to have sex? They are adults and are perfectly capable of making such decisions on their own.

The government mismanages the budget anyways, so what is the harm in evading taxes. It's a victimless crime and, anyway, everyone does it.

Sending your children over-seas to study is unpatriotic. Kids need to grow up here, in their home country, and get to know the traditions, customs and culture of their native country,

University students these days seem to care more about fashion and electronic gadgets than about social and political issues. Don't they see how shallow they are?

In today's ultra-competitive job market, it is acceptable to write a few exaggerations (even lies) in your resume. Everyone is doing it, so why shouldn't I?

Children belong to their parents. The government has no right to interfere in the way people bring up their children.

Having plastic surgery has become a fact of life for Korean women. They shouldn't be criticized for doing what they need to do to succeed.

Men have so much stress to cope with and they need to have some fun. Women shouldn't complain too much about their late nights, drinking, or even the occasional affair.

Discussion

1. Are you generally pessimistic or optimistic about human nature?

2. Do you think that you have a strong sense of right and wrong?

3. How do you determine what is right and wrong? (Parents, religion, friends...)

4. What holds you back from doing something you know is wrong? Are you afraid of getting caught? Does your conscience bother you?

5. Have you ever cheated on a test or exam? Did you feel guilty? Have you ever been caught? Have your friends ever cheated on a test or exam?

6. In today's **cutthroat** job market, is it necessary to '**embellish the truth**' a little on your resume, or in your job interview? Have you ever done it?

7. Have you ever stolen anything? Have you ever borrowed something and never returned it? Is it the same as stealing?

8. In your opinion, are you a hard worker, or do you **slack off** at school or work?

9. Have you ever gone to school or to work when you were drunk or badly hung-over? What happened?

10. Do you think sexual morals in your country are loosening up?

11. Are teenagers today more badly behaved than when you were a teenager? Why is this happening?

12. Are we getting too greedy and self-centered these days?

13. Have you ever **given in to peer pressure** and done something that you knew was wrong.

14. Have you ever **felt guilty** about doing something bad/wrong. Were you **remorseful**? Have you ever done something that made you feel ashamed?

15. Do you feel that most of your teachers have been **impartial**, or have some of them been biased in favor of some students?

16. Has a friend ever **confided in you** about something wrong that they have done? If yes, what had they done?

17. Do you **talk behind people's backs** very often? Can you remember a time when you found out that someone **had been talking behind your back**? How did you feel, and what did you do?

18. Has anyone **ever taken credit for** a project that you did most of the work on? Have you **taken credit for** someone else's work?

19. Do you ever volunteer your time to help the poor, the sick and the elderly?

20. Is it important for parents to **set a good moral and ethical example** for their children?

21. Should important company executives and CEOs guilty of unethical behavior – i.e., **evading taxes**, misusing or stealing company funds, tax fraud, etc. – face jail time? Or should this behavior be overlooked because of their overall contribution to the economy and job creation?

22. If your boss asked you to **falsify** information to help the company, would you do it?

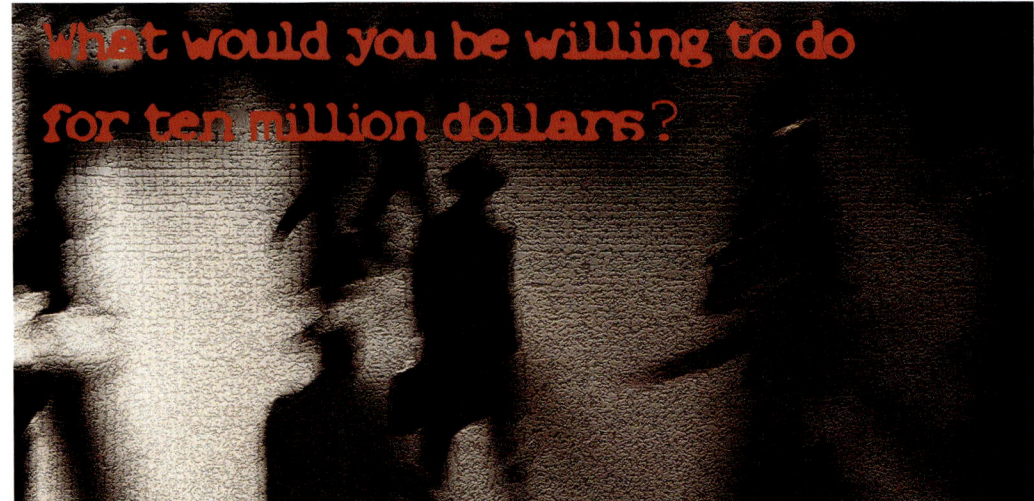

4 Diet and Exercise

Language Points

aerobic exercise / cardiovascular exercise / cardiovascular endurance

Going for a brisk run is really good cardiovascular exercise.

cosmetic

The majority of people in the gym exercise for cosmetic effects. They care mostly about looking slimmer, or most muscular, or younger. They care less about the health benefits.

excessive alcohol consumption / to drink excessively / to drink to excess

He drinks excessively. He gets drunk at least a couple of times a week.

to be in (good) shape / to be fit

He's in really good shape these days. He exercises at the gym several times a week, and eats nutritiously.

to be out of shape

He never works out anymore, and drinks too much beer. He's really out of shape.

couch potato

I was a real couch potato last weekend. I sat around watching television and eating snacks all weekend.

to put on weight / to gain weight / to lose weight

I've been gaining weight recently. I've put on three or four kilograms in the last few months. I feel so fat!

to go on a diet / to be on a diet / to be dieting / to diet

She's on a low-calorie diet because she's getting married next year and wants to look good in her wedding pictures. She's been dieting for a couple months now, and she's already looking slimmer.

health nut / health freak

He's a health nut. He eats three healthy meals every day, never smokes, exercises every day, and makes sure he gets a good sleep every night.

to watch what one eats

I try to watch what I eat because I want to stay healthy and slim. If I don't pay attention to what I'm eating, I'll eat too much junk food and I'll get fat and out of shape.

Reading

Fewer than 10 percent of American adults exercise four or more times a week, and more than half quit within six months of starting an exercise program. The same problems are true for children and teens: 52 percent of them do not exercise regularly. As a result, physical fitness standards have been falling. A recent test revealed that only 10 percent of high school students were rated healthy on a **cardiovascular** test. Add to that the growing hunger for fast food, and it is easy to see why doctors are worried about the future of today's adolescents and young adults.

With so many computer and video games to distract them, children seem to avoid good, old-fashioned exercise like running around on the playground or playing sports with their friends. Parents and guardians, too, may find it hard to make time for an evening jog or a quick game with the kids when there are interesting websites to surf on the Internet, programs to watch on TV, and films playing at the local movie theater.

Unfortunately, weight loss is usually the main reason women exercise and muscle tone is the main reason for men. Such **cosmetic** effects may take a long time to appear, discouraging people from continuing, even though the condition of their health is improving. The most important reason for exercising should be the health benefits exercise has for everyone.

Another thing that makes people less likely to exercise is the boredom of repetition. To many people, the thought of exercising means long hours on a **treadmill**, or endless repetitions on a weight bench. Exercise doesn't necessarily mean you have **to be cooped up** in the gym, though. There are other physical activities that many people find enjoyable, such as hiking, playing recreational sports, dancing, or biking. Also, exercising with other people or developing an interest or hobby that requires physical activity are likely to make any exercise **routine** much more pleasant.

With today's **hectic** lifestyle, it is easy to get caught in a cycle of unhealthy eating, laziness, bad sleeping habits, and **excessive alcohol consumption**. While we may not notice the effects of such habits immediately, they may become all too **apparent** in the future.

Comprehension

1. Can you summarize the reading passage in your own words?

2. What are some of the things that keep children and teens from exercising as much as they should?

3. Why does the author say that exercising to look good is a bad approach?

4. Does this article accurately describe the average lifestyle in your country? Why or why not?

Couch Potato Quiz

Answer these questions honestly with your classmate(s). Afterwards, decide whether or not you are a couch potato. What are some ways that you could change your lifestyle?

1. You're in the living room watching your favorite weekly TV show. Your Mom asks you to run out to the store to get some milk. How long would it take you to get up and go get it?

2. Do you ever spend the whole day on the couch watching TV, even when you aren't sick?

3. It's early on a Saturday morning and you've had a very rough Friday night. You are supposed to meet a group of friends for coffee. How late would you be?
   a) A few minutes
   b) At least an hour
   c) Are you kidding? I would call them and make an excuse not to go!

4. When you're sitting on your couch and the phone rings, do you:
   a) Race to the phone
   b) Tell your brother to get it
   c) Ignore it...if it is important, they'll leave a message.

5. Have you ever watched an exercise show without actually exercising?

6. Do you ever plan your day around what is on TV?

7. Do you have any take-out restaurant phone numbers memorized?

8. How often do beer and snacks replace a regular meal?

9. Do you panic when you misplace your remote control?

10. Do you have trouble renting a DVD because you have already watched everything good in the DVD store?

Fitness Assessment

Whenever you sign up for a membership at a health club or gym, a counselor interviews you about your fitness goals. You and your classmates will role-play this kind of fitness assessment. Take turns playing the part of the fitness counselor and the client, interviewing each other using the form below as a guideline. Discuss your current level of fitness, your fitness goals, and a plan that you could follow to achieve them.

What is your lifestyle like these days? Explain your answer.

☐ Mostly active   ☐ Moderately active   ☐ Mostly sedentary

How would you rate:

Your present cardiovascular capacity	① ② ③ ④ ⑤
Your present muscular capacity	① ② ③ ④ ⑤
Your present flexibility capacity	① ② ③ ④ ⑤

① Very Poor	② Poor	③ Average	④ Good	⑤ Very good

What kinds of exercise interest you? Which are you good at doing?

☐ Walking	☐ Jogging	☐ Swimming	☐ Cycling	☐ Dancing
☐ Aerobics	☐ Treadmill	☐ In-line skating	☐ Basketball	☐ Soccer
☐ Racquetball /Squash	☐ Strength Training	☐ Tennis	☐ Stationary Biking	☐ Other___

How much time are you willing to devote to an exercise program? Can you exercise during your workday? Would an exercise program interfere with your job?

What do you want exercise to do for you? Check all the boxes that apply. Then indicate their importance to you.

☐ Improve cardiovascular fitness	① ② ③ ④ ⑤
☐ Body-fat weight loss	① ② ③ ④ ⑤
☐ Reshape or tone my body	① ② ③ ④ ⑤
☐ Improve performance for a specific sport	① ② ③ ④ ⑤
☐ Improve moods and ability to cope with stress	① ② ③ ④ ⑤
☐ Improve flexibility	① ② ③ ④ ⑤
☐ Increase strength	① ② ③ ④ ⑤
☐ Increase energy level	① ② ③ ④ ⑤
☐ Feel better	① ② ③ ④ ⑤
☐ Enjoyment	① ② ③ ④ ⑤
☐ Other	① ② ③ ④ ⑤

①	②	③	④	⑤
Unimportant	Somewhat unimportant	Average	Somewhat important	Very important

Lifestyles of the Soft and Flabby

Work with your classmate(s). From each pair of items, choose one and explain why you would choose it. Instead of explaining that you chose something just because you like it, try to explain why you like it more.

Delicious, fattening food	Tasteless, healthy food
Watching a movie with friends	Going for a walk with friends
Eating whatever you want	Watching what you eat
Taking the elevator up three floors	Walking up three flights of stairs
A soft drink	Juice or water
Going to the bar	Going to the gym
Smoking	Not smoking
Snack food	Celery or carrot sticks
Driving to do your errands	Bicycling to do your errands
Drinking alcohol	Not drinking alcohol
Donuts	Whole wheat bread
Ice cream	Fruit
Hamburger and Fries	Vegetable sandwiches

1. Is regular exercise essential for health and happiness?

2. **Are you in good (or excellent) shape**? Are you in better or worse shape than the average person? How do you stay/keep in shape?

3. **Are you out of shape**? Do you think you need to **lose weight**? Have you **been putting on/gaining weight** recently? Do you blame your **hectic lifestyle**, or is that just an excuse? How do you plan to get in shape? What could you do to improve your health?

4. Do you like working out at the gym or in health clubs, or do you find it boring? Are they too expensive?

5. When you go to the gym, do you go mostly for the health benefits or the **cosmetic** effects?

6. What kinds of **aerobic** and **cardiovascular exercise** do you get? Do you ever take a jazz dance, aerobics, a kickboxing, or yoga class? Would you like to?

7. What sports do you play? How often? What sport would you like to learn or participate in?

8. Do you do any other physical activities, such as hiking in the mountains, cycling, swimming, etc?

9. Do you **watch what you eat**? Do you eat three healthy meals a day? Do you often skip meals? Do you usually (or always) skip breakfast?

10. Is there anything you like eating or drinking that isn't good for you? Do you eat too many unhealthy snacks? Do you eat a lot of fast food and junk food? Are you worried that your bad eating habits are going to catch up with you when you are older?

11. Have you ever gone on a diet? What did you eat? What did you avoid?

12. Is there anything you can't or won't eat or drink? What food do you try to avoid?

13. Do you know somebody who's always on a diet or has a strange diet?

14. Do you sometimes **drink to excess**? How will this affect your health in the future? Do you have any plans to cut back on these bad habits?

15. Do you take vitamins and other health tonics?

16. Have all our modern conveniences (i.e., cars, computers, etc.) made us a lot lazier?

17. Do you think that people put too much emphasis on being thin, without regard for being healthy?

18. Do you have too much stress in your life? Does stress have a negative effect on your life? How do you relieve stress?

19. What do you think is the most serious health problem in your country? What are the main causes?

20. Of all the people you know, who leads the healthiest lifestyle? And the least healthy lifestyle? What are their lifestyles like?

LESSON

5 Asking For and Receiving Advice

to offer someone advice about something

I don't think I could offer you any useful advice about which car to buy.

to get someone's opinion about / on something

Why don't you get my brother's opinion on it?

to suggest / recommend (that) someone (should) do something

He might recommend that you look for a good used car.

to suggest / recommend something (to someone)

He'd probably suggest a used Ford Mustang.

to suggest / recommend doing something

I recommend bringing it to my cousin Mark's garage. You can trust him.

If I were you / in your situation / in your shoes, I would ...

If I were you, I wouldn't buy an imported car. The repairs are expensive.

Have you (ever) considered / thought about something / doing something?

Have you considered buying a Ford? They're quite reliable.

You might try doing something.

You might try looking on some of the used car sites on the Internet.

Dialogue

Two friends are talking at a local pub.

John: Didn't you say that you wanted to ask me about something?

Arnold: Yeah. It's a little bit embarrassing, though. Are you sure you don't mind? **I wouldn't be offended if you didn't want to talk about it.**

John: Come on. What are friends for? What's up?

Arnold: I've decided that it's time I got married. But I just can't seem to meet the right woman. What do you think I should do?

John: (Laughing) I don't think you'll have much luck finding the right woman, because I've already married her.

Arnold: (Groaning) Seriously, though. What am I doing wrong?

John: Well, personally, I think you should shave off your beard. What possessed you to grow a beard?! You're only 36. **If you didn't have a beard, I think women would definitely find you more attractive.**

Arnold: Really?

John: Definitely. And another thing; what's up with the way you dress these days? You look like you just rolled out of bed with all your clothes on. Ever heard of ironing?

Arnold: Give me a break, man; **I'd iron my clothes if I had more time.** But you know what it's like at work these days. I barely have enough time to breathe.

John:	Well, I'm just telling you that you're not going to find Miss Right looking like something the cat dragged in off the street. **If you got yourself cleaned up, I'm sure you'd have a lot more luck.** And what's with that beer belly? You used to be a lot slimmer. You've really let yourself go.
Arnold:	Yeah, you're right. The truth is that I do have enough time to look after myself. It's just that I've been sort of down since Heather and I broke up. Things were going really well between us.
John:	Didn't the two of you see each other for, like, two years?
Arnold:	Yeah, **we wouldn't have broken it off, either, if she hadn't been transferred to Syracuse**.
John:	**I bet she'd be happy to hear from you if you called her.** Why don't you? It wouldn't hurt to try.
Arnold:	You're right. Actually, **I would've called her weeks ago, if I hadn't lost her new number.** My place is a disaster.
John:	(Rolling his eyes.) Oh, boy. Get it together, man.

Comprehension

1. What sort of advice does Arnold ask John for?

2. What is John's advice?

3. What did Arnold's real problem turn out to be?

4. What would you tell Arnold to do if you were John?

5. How can you express the sentence 'It wouldn't hurt to try' in a different way?

Activity A

A Panel of Experts

Decide on two fields or topics that you think you know something about. Write your fields of expertise on a piece of paper and put it in front of you on the desk so that all of the other members of the group can see it. Each member of the group will then take turns asking for advice from one of the experts in the group. You may ask one question per turn. Below are some fields or topics you might consider choosing as your 'fields of expertise'.

Love & Sex	Relationships	Money
Career Planning	Travel	Self-improvement
Home Decorating	Education	Computers
Raising Children	Retirement	Socializing
Etiquette	Sports	Investments
Studying Abroad	Alcohol	Cooking
Business	Real Estate	Cars
Psychology	Women	Men

Role Play

Discuss the following situations with your classmate(s). Take turns pretending to be the person described and asking for advice.

1 You work for the president of a very large corporation, but he's always losing his temper and swearing at people. It is really testing your patience.

2 You have just started dating someone, and they seem perfect except for their terrible breath.

3 One of your neighbors keeps parking behind your car, but never leaves his car in neutral so you can push it out of the way when you need to leave. You've told him about it twice now, and he hasn't got the message. Now you are thinking about taking a baseball bat to his windshield.

4 A friend is always borrowing small amounts of money from you, but she never pays you back. At first, it didn't bother you, but now it's becoming a habit.

5 Your boss asked you to work late and finish a very important report. When an old friend of yours called you up, you forgot about the report and went out drinking with him. Your boss is giving a presentation today and needs that report.

6 You went to a new hair salon to get your hair cut, but the inexperienced hairdresser accidentally cut a large chunk out of your bangs.

7 Your daughter is 11 years old and is still wetting her bed. You have scolded her about this situation but it only seems to make things worse.

8 You are trying to save money for some big purchases, but it seems to be hard these days just to make ends meet.

9 Life is getting you down these days. You have figured out that the main reason is that you don't have enough time to spend with your friends. Life seems so hectic, though, and you don't know how you would find the time.

In Dire Straits

Below you will find some letters written to an advice column, and some of the responses that have been proposed. Together with your classmate(s), choose the best and the worst advice and explain why you chose it. Alternatively, give your own advice.

Letters

Dear Shelly,

I really want to travel this summer, but I don't have enough money. What should I do?
- Wanderlust
  in Detroit

Dear Shelly,

No matter how hard I try, I can't seem to find a job. It's been four months since I started looking and I'm starting to get really discouraged.
- Willing and Able
  in Los Angeles

Dear Shelly,

My mother-in-law lives in the same building and is always dropping by unannounced. She comes by almost every day, and it's driving me crazy. Why can't she just leave us alone!
- Unwilling Hostess
  in New York

Dear Shelly,

I don't know what's come over me! For weeks now, I've been feeling really blue. It just doesn't make sense. My life's going alright, so why do I always feel like I'm on the verge of tears?
- Down in the Dumps
  in Cincinnati

Advice

Dear *Wanderlust*,

1. Just use your credit cards and go away for a short break.
2. Hold-off until you have saved up enough money for a really great vacation.
3. Just take a couple of short, cheap domestic trips.
4. Other

Dear *Willing and Able*,

1. You must be doing something wrong. Change your approach.
2. Four months is nothing! Stop whining and keep trying!
3. How about just taking a low-paid job for now?
4. Other

Dear *Unwilling Hostess*,

1. Don't put up with it! Just tell her to stop hassling you!
2. Unfortunately, mother-in-laws are part of the deal when you get married - get used to it!
3. Why don't you get your husband to talk to her?
4. Other

Dear *Down in the Dumps*,

1. How about finding a new hobby or making some new friends?
2. Don't take this the wrong way, but maybe you need to see a professional.
3. It'll pass. In the meantime, you should find someone you trust to talk to.
4. Other

6 Feelings and Emotions

Language Points

to feel uptight / anxious
> I'm sorry I snapped at you. I'm feeling really uptight about things at work.

to take a toll
> Actually, my stress at work is also taking its toll on my family life.

to have no patience for something
> I have no patience for my coworkers.

to go ballistic
> Sometimes, I just go ballistic and start yelling at them!

to control one's emotions
> I know I should control my emotions, but I can't help myself.

to be at the end of one's rope
> I've tried everything, and now I'm at the end of my rope.

to get a grip
> My manager just tells me to get a grip or I'll lose my job.

to blow off steam
> Let's go out tonight. I need to blow off a little steam.

to lighten up
> Everything is going to be alright. Stop worrying and lighten up. Why don't you have a glass of wine? It will help lighten you up.

Dialogue

Two university students talk about their grades.

Eric: How's it going, Steven?

Steven: To tell you the truth, not too well. I'm **feeling** really **uptight** these days. As you know, it's exam time and I've been studying around the clock for over a week. I think all this work is finally **taking its toll** on me.

Eric: What do you mean?

Steven: Well, for starters, **I have no patience** for my little brother. I **went ballistic** this afternoon when he came into my room and asked me to play with him. I even threw him out and slammed the door. This upset my mother, who then told me not to be so moody and to **control my emotions**. Don't they know I'm studying for exams?

Eric: You sound as though you've reached **the end of your rope**.

Steven: I have to admit I've been very **edgy** the last couple of days, but there's nothing I can do about it right now.

Eric: I think there are a few things you can do to help yourself in this situation.

You're looking rather **gaunt**, so I hope you've been eating properly. If you maintain good eating habits, you'll maintain a healthy mind. Also, you've got to try to get enough rest. You can't expect to study effectively if you're tired.

Steven: But when I try to sleep, I just **toss and turn** because I'm so worried about failing.

Eric: Well, if you don't **get a grip** on things, you won't be passing anything. You're going to have to **lighten up** a little. I suggest you go back home and apologize to your mother and brother. Believe it or not, your brother was really trying to help you. You should have taken a few minutes to play with him and gotten your mind off your studies.

Steven: Thanks for the advice. I know you're right. I guess I just needed to **blow off steam**. I've got to run. See you after exams.

Comprehension

1. What problem does Steven describe to his friend?

2. What advice does Eric offer him?

3. Do you think this is useful advice?

4. What would you have recommended he do?

Vocabulary Focus

Fill in the blanks with the correct expression from the box.

to lighten up	to blow off some steam	to control one's emotions
to go ballistic	to get a grip on	taking its toll
feeling uptight	to have no patience	pale

1. He was as white as a ghost. He looked so_____.

2. When I told my father I got into an accident with his car, he _____.

3. Her boss turned down her request for a raise so she went out drinking after work to _____.

4. When her boyfriend didn't call her for two days, she got very upset. She has to learn _____.

5. He was under a lot of stress and couldn't eat or sleep. If he doesn't _____ the situation, he will need to take time off work.

6. Her boyfriend was about to propose to her. He was really _____.

7. He hasn't been getting enough sleep, nor has he been eating properly for over a month. I think its _____on him because now he's complaining of stomach problems.

8. I wish my boss would _____ a bit. He never laughs and goes around the office with a frown on his face all day.

9. His professor _____ for people who handed in their reports late.

Anger Management

When something or someone starts to get under your skin do you tend to let your feelings show or keep your feelings to yourself? When you start to feel your anger levels rise do you typically try to control your feelings or do you let rip? Choose one of the positions below and debate the advantages and disadvantages of each approach with your partner.

POSITION ONE - EXPRESSION	POSITION TWO - REPRESSION
• Showing your displeasure is the fastest and most effective way to resolve a problem	• Staying calm is the best way to think rationally
• Some people only really take you seriously if you get angry	• Adopting a diplomatic approach is the best way to stop a situation **getting out of hand**
• Venting your anger is better for your health than **bottling-up your feelings**	• 9 out of 10 of the things we say in anger we later regret
• Letting others know that you are unhappy about something is the best way to **assert yourself**	• If you **rant and rave** too much, people are likely to think you are high maintenance and try to avoid you
• **Getting tough** from the start is the best way to discourage others from messing with you in the future	• Sometimes it is better to **keep your opinions to yourself**
• Not only will other people respect you if you **lose it** once in a while but you will respect yourself	• You can appear to be easy-going and people will like you

Bottling-up your feelings - not showing your emotions
Assert yourself - express your opinion directly
Getting tough - dealing with a situation without compromise
Lose it - lose your temper, get really angry
Getting out of hand - getting out of control
Rant and rave - shout loudly and angrily
Keep your opinions to yourself - think something but don't say it

Aggravations and Amusements

Explain how you would react to the following situations. Focus on describing how you might feel in each case and how you would respond.

- You accidentally lock your car with the keys inside.
- You have come to a great restaurant with your boyfriend/girlfriend in the hope of having a perfect meal. But the waiter is an ex-boyfriend/girlfriend.
- You have been taking an English conversation class and during one activity you accidentally make a mistake that makes everyone laugh, including the instructor.
- Your company or university offers you the chance to do a nine-month special course in California. You will, however, have to be away from your parents, friends, and family.

- You are running to catch a bus. The driver pulls away, just as you reach the door.
- You have just had a blind date with someone who seems to be absolutely perfect for you.
- You are out shopping and you make eye contact with someone you know quite well, but they just walk past you without saying a word.
- You have just finished eating a delicious, but expensive meal. You ask for the bill. The waiter brings it, but the bill is much smaller than you were expecting because he has forgotten to include several items that you have eaten.
- You get home after a long day, only to find that there is nowhere to park your car.
- You are eating lunch with your boss and a colleague you really dislike. During the meal, the colleague accidentally knocks over a tall glass of ice water, and it ends up in your boss's lap.
- You are having a nice conversation with your friend on the subway when an elderly man tells you in an angry voice that it is a public place, and you are disturbing him by speaking too loudly.
- You and your best friend had a big argument a couple of days ago. You thought your friendship was finished. But then your friend called you on the telephone, apologized, and asked for your forgiveness.
- You are having dinner with a friend when someone at the next table suddenly collapses on the floor.
- You have agreed to meet your friend for dinner at your favorite restaurant. When you arrive at the restaurant, everyone shouts, "Surprise!" It is a huge surprise birthday party for you. All of your best friends and favorite relatives are there.
- As you walk by a group of young people, you notice that they are laughing amongst themselves and pointing at you.
- You go to a new restaurant in your neighborhood. After you have been seated and open the menu, you find the prices are much higher than you'd thought.
- You are on a crowded subway and a seat becomes available right in front of you. As you turn around to sit down, a speedy middle-aged woman darts into the vacant seat.

Activity C

The Way I Feel

1 What makes you feel ecstatic?
2 What makes you nervous?
3 What relaxes you?
4 What makes you feel furious?
5 What gives you stress?
6 What makes you feel proud?
7 What frustrates you?
8 What makes you jealous or envious?
9 What gives you a sense of satisfaction?
10 What makes you laugh?

A. Work alone. Take a few minutes and write a list for each emotion. Try to write a few things for each emotion.

B. Work with a partner or in a small group. Compare and discuss your lists with the lists of your partner(s). Make a group list containing the best ideas, or the ones that you all agree on.

C. *Either* explain your group's ideas to the class, *or* form new groups and compare your lists. Do they agree with you? Do they have other suggestions?

Discussion

1. Are you embarrassed when you are praised in front of other people? What do you usually do when this happens? What do you usually say?

2. What was the happiest day of your life? What was the most disappointing day of your life? Describe what happened, and why you felt the way you did.

3. At what time of day are you in your best mood? At what time of day are you in your worst mood? Why?

4. Can you remember a time when you, one of your friends, or one of your relatives **went ballistic**? Or failed to **control your/their emotions**? Can you remember a time when you saw somebody you didn't know **go ballistic**?

5. When you feel angry or stressed, how do you **blow off steam**?

6. Are you **feeling uptight** or **anxious** about anything these days?

7. Do you think money can buy happiness? Do you need money to be happy?

8. Which is more important to you: Success or happiness?

9. Are you a naturally optimistic or pessimistic person?

10. When you're feeling down, what do you do to cheer yourself up?

11. What would make you feel really happy these days? What is missing from your life that would make you incredibly happy? Why?

12. As you get older, are you becoming happier? In general, do you think that people become happier as they get older?

13. In general, who do you think are happier: married people, people with a boyfriend/girlfriend, or single people? Men or women? High school students or university students?

14. Are the people in your home country generally happy?

15. What has been the happiest period of your life?

16. Which of the following things are most responsible for the level of happiness that people feel: friends, socializing, marriage, money, health, genes (genetic factors), work, experiencing something new, age.

17. What is the funniest thing you've seen or heard recently? What's the funniest thing you've ever seen or heard?

18. Are you good at hiding your emotions or do you wear your heart on your sleeve?

7 On My Conscience

Language Points

to go easy on someone
> My teenage son constantly disobeys us, and he always does the opposite of what we tell him, but we don't punish him harshly. We go easy on him.

to give someone a good talking to
> We worry about him staying out late, drinking, and smoking. We've tried giving him a good talking to, but he just ignores us.

to ground someone
> Maybe we need to give him a harsher punishment and ground him. If he couldn't leave the house for one week, maybe he would learn the lesson.

to give someone a good belting
> We've never felt the need to resort to physical discipline before, but maybe we should give him a good belting.

to be lenient with someone
> Maybe our son's poor behavior is our own fault. We've been too lenient with him in the past.

socially acceptable
> Politicians in many countries tax tobacco, but they do not tax alcohol because drinking is much more socially acceptable than smoking.

an unwritten (social) rule
> In conservative countries there is an unwritten social rule against kissing in public, but in liberal countries it is socially acceptable.

anti-social / anti-social behavior
> Burping loudly in public is antisocial.

social graces
> People who burp loudly in public and spit on the sidewalk lack social graces.

a guilty conscience
> I have a guilty conscience whenever I skip English class.

on (my/your/his/her) conscience
> My conscience is troubled by the unkind things I said to her. I'm going to call her and apologize. I've had it on my conscience for weeks.

ease (my/your) my conscience
> I eased my conscience by telling my boss about the big mistake that I had made and covered up.

Dialogue

Two young mothers are talking outside of a house.

Jen: Oh, hi there, Amy. Wow! Your little Andy is really growing up fast, isn't he? Seems like just the other day you were pushing him around in the **pram**! Now, just look at him running around with all the other kids. He looks like he's **having a blast**!

Amy: Sure, but he's a handful. He's got so much energy. **If I take my eyes off him for even a second, he's gone like a flash.** I didn't know having children would be so...exhausting. I wish Andy were as well behaved as your little one.

Jen: Robbie? Yeah, I guess he's usually pretty good. **Mind you**, my husband and I have really worked at it - right **from square one**.

Amy: What's your secret?

Jen: Well, actually, we've just changed the way we discipline him. **When Robbie did something wrong, my husband used to spank him.**

Amy: Really? But most of the parenting books say spanking isn't an effective way. I thought it just gives children low self-esteem.

Jen: Well, that's what I told my husband. But he was so sure of what he was doing. It's because of the way he was raised. **Whenever he was bad, his father used to beat him.**

Amy: Oh, that's horrible.

Jen: I know, nice, huh? But then we saw this show on TV about this child psychologist in the States. He said that, **unless it's explained to them, children don't necessarily understand what they've done wrong. If you tell them, they understand why they have to stop.**

Amy: Well, maybe after the 57th time!

Jen: That's what we thought too, but we tried his method and, you know, it really works. Now, **whenever he does something wrong, we sit him down and talk to him about what he did and why it's wrong.** Then we give him a hug.

Amy: Huh. We'll have to try that.

Jen: **If he doesn't do it the next time, we shower him with praise. So now, we spank him only if he's doing something over and over again.**

Amy: Well, that makes sense to me. I'll have to talk to my husband about it.

Jen: Sorry, Amy. We'd better get going. Robbie's got to have his nap pretty soon or he'll start getting moody. Nice chatting with you.

Amy: Yeah, maybe we'll see you here tomorrow.

1. What are the two women talking about?

2. What does Amy mean when she says, "maybe after the 57th time"?

3. How do Jen and her husband discipline their child?

4. Why did they change their method of disciplining him?

5. Do you agree with what the child psychologist said?

6. Which of the following opinions do you agree with?

- Sometimes, parents face situations in which physical punishment is the only alternative.
- Teachers have the job of educating children. If physical punishment is necessary, teachers should use it.
- Teachers have no right to discipline children, especially physically.
- Children belong to their parents. The government has no right to interfere in the way people bring up their children.
- Children should be allowed to run wild until they go to school…and their lives become hell.

- Spare the rod, spoil the child. Punishing children is an act of love, and by not punishing them for doing wrong, you are running their character.
- All forms of physical punishment are abusive and should be illegal. There is no excuse for hitting children.
- Spanking helps children remember important lessons. It's more effective than saying the same thing 10 times.
- Disciplining children lowers their self-esteem. They should be allowed to discover the negative consequences of their actions on their own.

Parenting F.A.Q.s

The following are letters that have been written to the parenting columnist at a local newspaper. She is on vacation, and you and your classmate(s) have to come up with answers to be written up for the column. Discuss the problems and try to come up with the best advice for these desperate parents.

Undercover Puffer

I have a fourteen-year-old daughter who has been coming home lately smelling of cigarette smoke. When I questioned her she said that she had been hanging out with some older friends who were smoking. At the time I warned her about the dangers of smoking and she assured me that she wouldn't smoke. However, the other day a friend of mine saw my daughter smoking with friends in a coffee shop. Despite that, she still denied it. What should I do?

The Neighbourhood Nibbler

My 3-and-a-half-year-old girl, Tamara, is a sweetheart, but is sometimes a 'biter'. This started when she was two years old, when she started biting her older sister during quarrels. But lately, she's started biting other kids on the playground when she doesn't get her way. I want to curb this behaviour before she goes to school. I am in need of some help.

Midnight Mischief

Recently my teenage son has been staying up all hours using the Internet. As a result it's almost impossible to get him out of bed in the morning and he is always complaining about having no energy during the day. On top of that, his schoolwork seems to be suffering. I keep telling him to get to bed a reasonable time but he doesn't take any notice of me. The other night when I walked in his room I caught him viewing hard-core pornography! I'm desperate - please help!

Busy Signal

Rebecca was doing fine in school until she hit the 10th grade. Now she seems to have lost all her motivation. She spends most of her weeknights on the phone to her friends. She hasn't been open with us about it, but we suspect that she has a boyfriend. What should we do? I want her to understand that working hard in school is important for her future!

Brash Brat

I got a phone call the other day from my son's high school teacher saying that he has been absent from school on average 1 day per week this term. When I confronted him about it he just shrugged his shoulders and said 'what's the big deal, everyone does it'. 'Anyway', he says ' it's all stuff I've learned at the institute already'. I've tried reasoning with him but it doesn't seem to work.

Activity B

Do You Feel Guilty When...

A. When was the last time you felt guilty about doing something? What did you do? Why did you feel guilty? Discuss with a partner or in a small group.

B. Which of these things leave you with a guilty conscience? What do you do to ease your conscience? Discuss with a partner or in a small group.

1. Throwing litter on the street
2. Wasting a lot of paper
3. Throwing glass and plastic bottles, aluminum cans, and paper into the trash bin, instead of recycling them
4. Laughing at someone because they have made a mistake
5. Taking long showers
6. Driving a gas-guzzling car
7. Forgetting the birthday of someone important to you (a close relative, friend, girlfriend, boyfriend, spouse, etc.)
8. Telling a white lie to someone important to you (a close relative, friend, girlfriend, boyfriend, spouse, etc.)
9. Telling a big lie to someone important to you
10. Not doing your homework (and lying to your teacher about the reason)
11. Cheating on a test
12. Smoking in a no-smoking area
13. Accepting credit for something that you didn't actually do
14. Letting your cell phone ring at the movie theater
15. Keeping people waiting for about 10 minutes; for more than 30 minutes
16. Spending a lot of money on yourself
17. Stealing office supplies from your company or school
18. Talking about people behind their back
19. Listening to other people's private conversations on the street, on the subway, or in a restaurant or café
20. Reading other people's text messages over their shoulders while they are on the subway
21. _____

C. Tell the class which behaviors you and your partner(s) are guilty of, and what (if anything) you do to ease your conscience.

Some People Have a Lot of Nerve!

Somewhere along the line, rude people were not taught better ways of behaving. Look at the list below. Discuss these behaviors with a partner. Which ones are socially unacceptable? Which ones have become (or are becoming) socially acceptable? Use the questions in the box as a guide for your conversation.

- How often do people...?
- Do you consider it rude when people...?
- Why does it annoy you when someone...?
- How does it make you feel when people...?
- What do you think of people who...?
- How do you react when someone...?
- Which behaviors are **socially unacceptable**...?
- Which ones have become (or are becoming) **socially acceptable**...?

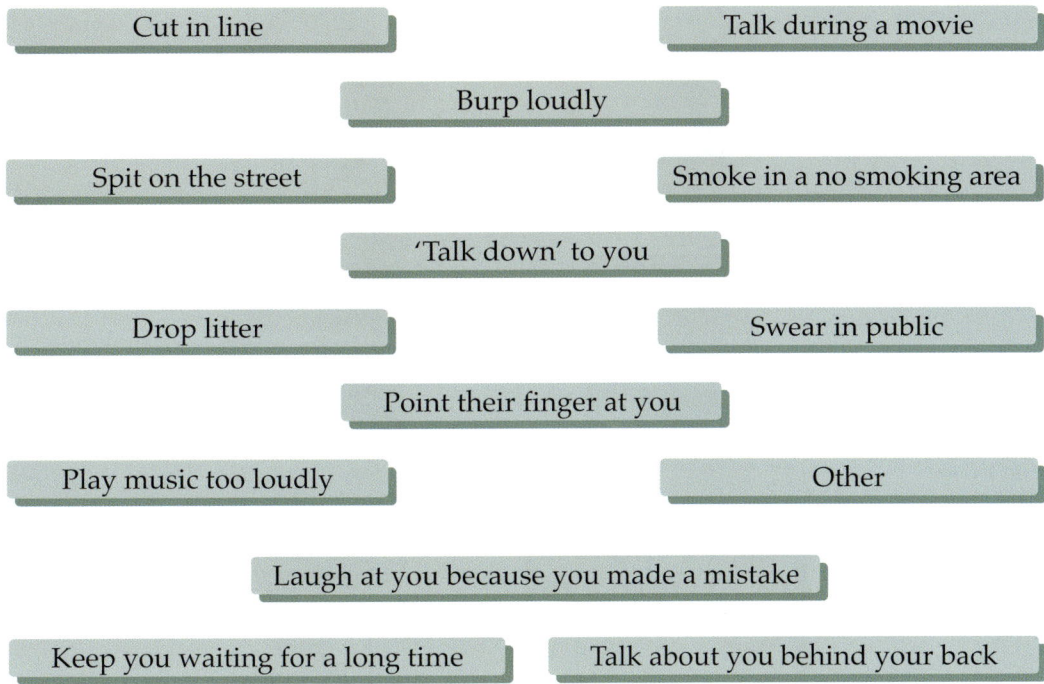

Cut in line

Talk during a movie

Burp loudly

Spit on the street

Smoke in a no smoking area

'Talk down' to you

Drop litter

Swear in public

Point their finger at you

Play music too loudly

Other

Laugh at you because you made a mistake

Keep you waiting for a long time

Talk about you behind your back

Activity D

Signs

A. Match the sign to the place(s) where you are most likely to find it. Put the numbers of the signs that match each place in the blank.

Places

- **The loading area by a storefront**

- **A public parking lot**

- **A convenience store**

- **A public swimming pool**

- **A crosswalk**

- **A highway**

- **A subway station/platform**

- **A park**

- **Movie theatre**

① ② ③

④ ⑤ ⑥

⑦ PROPER ID REQUIRED
We do NOT sell cigarettes to persons under the age of 19.

⑧ UNAUTHORIZED VEHICLES WILL BE TOWED AWAY AT OWNER'S EXPENSE

⑨ TOW AWAY ZONE

⑩ Arrive Alive Don't Drink & Drive!

⑫ 18ᴬ Persons younger than 18 must be accompanied by an adult

⑪ DISABLED PARKING TOWING ENFORCED / MAXIMUM FINE $500

B. Find the signs that the following sentences refer to. Complete the gaps with verbs in the box. More than one verb is possible for many sentences. You will have to write the negative form in some cases. Compare your answers with a partner.

are allowed to	can	have to	must
need to	should	may	

❶ You _____ park your car here.

❷ You _____ park your car here unless you are handicapped.

❸ You _____ present proper identification to buy cigarettes.

4 You _____ dive into the pool.

5 You _____ keep your dog on a leash.

6 You _____ be careful crossing the street.

7 You _____ wear your seat belt.

8 You _____ stand too close to the tracks.

9 You _____ use your cell phone in the theatre.

10 You _____ never drive drunk.

C. **Which rules do you agree with? Which rules do you always follow? Which rules are unnecessary and annoying? Which rules do you break frequently?**

D. **Work with a partner or in a small group. Make a list of rules (written rules and unwritten rules) that apply to the places below. Also, write some rules that have not been made yet, but which you think should be made to preserve public morals at each location.**

- **airports and flying**
- **roadways and driving**
- **libraries and classrooms**
- **your city or country**
- **your place of work**
- **dating**

Discussion

1. What were some of the rules your parents had for you when you were young? What were the **consequences** of breaking them?

2. Did you have any **chores** to do? Were you rewarded for doing them?

3. What were some of the methods of punishment that your parents used? Did they ever use physical punishment?

4. Do you think that your parents were too **strict** or too **lenient**? Why?

5. Would (or do) you raise your children the way your parents raised you? Why or why not?

6. What are some of the most important lessons that you want to teach your own children? How will you teach them these things?

7. When your children **misbehave**, what methods do you (will you) use to correct them? Are these methods effective? Give some examples.

8. What are some things that your parents did that you would never do? What are some things that you have seen other parents do that you would never do?

9. What are some things that you would allow your children to do that other parents may not allow their children to do?

10. Would you teach your child to hit back at school if somebody hits them?

11. What do you think of physical punishment? How much is appropriate? What methods are acceptable? What methods are not?

12. What is the difference between appropriate physical punishment and **child abuse**?

13. In some countries, it is illegal for parents to hit their children in public. Do you agree with this sort of law? Why or why not?

14. Are there child abuse laws in your country? Are they **stringent** enough? Are they properly **enforced**?

15. In English-speaking culture, there is a saying - "Spare the rod, spoil the child." Do you agree with this?

16. In many countries, teachers are not permitted to use physical punishment on students for any reason. Because of this, some say, students are not **obedient**. What other sorts of punishments can teachers give students?

17. Do you think that parents are too lenient with their children these days? What makes you think so?

18. What do you think are some of the most difficult problems faced by parents?

19. When you went to school, were teachers permitted to use **corporal** (physical) punishment on students? Describe a typical example. Were you ever physically disciplined at school?

20. Punishment: What would you do if you found out your child …

> … was shoplifting (stealing)?
> … had told you a big lie?
> … had been bullying other students?
> … had skipped school for a day?
> … had been rude to his teachers?
> … was visiting pornographic websites?

In which cases would you be **lenient** and **go easy on the child**? When would you **give the child a good talking to**? When would you **ground** the child? And when, if ever, would you **give the child a good belting**? What other forms of punishment would be appropriate for each case?

LESSON 8

What's Your Line of Work?

Language Points

to apply for a job

Now that I have graduated from university, I am going to apply for a job. If I get it, I hope to begin work soon, and begin earning some money.

to be qualified for a job

I am well qualified for the job that I am applying for. I have the educational background and the work experience that the company is looking for.

to be fired / get fired

I was fired from my last job because I made a lot of mistakes and sometimes fell asleep on the job. My manager hated me.

to work in a field

I have more than 20 years' work experience in the IT field, so I feel that I am well-qualified for a job at a technology company.

to work (for a company) (as a position) (in a department)

I'm working for G.E. as a sales representative in the call center.

work full-time / part-time

Her husband works full-time because he needs to earn a lot of money, but she works only part-time because she needs to take care of their child.

self-motivated

I am self-motivated. I always make plans and complete assignments without my manager's direction.

a self-starter

I am a self-starter, so my manager never has to ask me to begin work on a project.

to make good money / the money is good / the money is great

In many western countries, a skilled plumber or carpenter can make good money. They often make better money than a university professor.

Dialogue

Two friends meet at a bar.

Hank:	Sorry I'm a little late. I **got caught up** in traffic.
Dino:	No problem. I just got here a few minutes ago myself.
Hank:	Have we got enough time to eat before going to the game? We won't have to rush, will we?
Dino:	Don't worry. It's only 6:10. The game doesn't start until quarter to eight and it only takes 15 minutes to get there.
Hank:	Great. Let's order. I haven't had time to eat anything since breakfast. I'm **famished**... So, how are things? How's the job search going?

Dino: Well, I've had two **job offers**. One's for a job here in New York with Bateman Securities, and the other is for a job in Boston. Both are in the financial field.

Hank: Two job offers. That's fantastic! But Boston? I didn't know you were thinking of moving. Have you made a decision yet about which job you're going to take?

Dino: I'm still undecided but I'm kind of **leaning towards** the one in Boston. It's with a multinational company called Long and King Associates. It's an interesting position. I'd be doing a lot of overseas travel, plus I'd be my own boss, drive a company car and set my own schedule.

Hank: If you take that job you'll be away from your family and all your friends. When will they get to see you?

Dino: I know, I know. Maybe I shouldn't even consider it, but the money is great and the travel is exciting. Maybe I should just stay here, though. That way I would have my family and friends close by. I'd hate to leave.

Hank: Are there any other reasons for taking the job here in New York?

Dino: They're offering more money, and, with a new baby on the way, I do have to buy a bigger car. It's a hard decision.

Hank: When do they want an answer from you?

Dino: Bateman wants me to respond the day after tomorrow. I have until next week to **get back to** Long and King.

Hank: If you want, we can stay here and talk about it some more, but it's almost time to go.

Dino: I think we'd better get to the game. Maybe it'll help me take my mind off the problem. I'm sure that after some relaxation, I'll be able to look at the situation from a better perspective.

Hank: Sounds good. Let's **hustle** or we'll miss the opening pitch.

Comprehension

1. What are Dino and Hank talking about?

2. How many job offers has Dino received? What are the pros and cons of each one?

3. Which one does it seem like Dino will most likely take? What makes you think so?

4. Which one would you choose?

Activity A

The Right Person for the Job

Work in groups. You work in the Human Resources Department of a large resort chain, Club Caribbean. You and your classmates are a committee making a decision about which of the four candidates you have interviewed is most suitable for the position. First read the advertisement below concerning a trainee position that is open at Club Caribbean. You and the members of your group must agree on one candidate for this position. Your group should rank each candidate from 1 (ideal) to 4 (least desirable).

Opening: Administrative Trainee

International resort chain is seeking a self-motivated university graduate for a future management position in the hospitality industry. The applicant must be ambitious and a self-starter. Should enjoy meeting and pleasing clients. Good communication skills are a must. Previous related experience and a working ability in a foreign language are desired but not essential. Must be willing to travel and change work locations on short notice. Please forward your resume by e-mail to Marquee Personnel at marpr01@hanmail.net.

NAME	Marissa Smith	John Jacobs	Kent Myers	Nancy Bateman
AGE	26	31	27	22
MARITAL STATUS	Divorced	Married with two children	Single	Single
UNIVERSITY	University of Michigan	Duke University	Yale University	Michigan State University
MAJOR	Nutrition	Social Work	Business Administration	Elementary Education
GRADE POINT AVERAGE	4.0	3.95	2.8	3.4
WORK HISTORY	Works in a beauty salon. Previously worked part-time in a convenience store.	Work experience with many NGOs as a caseworker. Has had two periods of unemployment. Worked in an orphanage for two years.	Just graduated and has never held a job. No volunteer work.	Worked at a camp for needy children. Tutored students in math while in university. Worked as a part-time babysitter.
ABILITIES	English and some French. Some business skills.	Experience with database management. Good writing skills.	Knowledge of many software programs. No language skills besides English.	Speaks fluent Chinese. Spreadsheet skills.
PERSONAL COMMENTS	I'm interested in starting a real career with a big company. I have good people skills. I can communicate with various kinds of customers. I am free to travel.	I am able to help people who need assistance. I would love a job that provides stability and a steady paycheck. My children are young and want me to have a good career.	The training program will teach me management skills. I will learn a foreign language on my own sometime in the future. I love to travel. I think I can deal with most business problems. I have excellent communication skills with females.	I am young and enthusiastic. I want to be part of a successful business. I love helping clients, especially children. I am afraid of flying but will try it if required.

Have You Ever Thought about Being a ...?

1. Choose a few occupations from the list below:

- civil servant
- university professor
- surgeon
- restaurant owner
- English instructor
- defense lawyer
- prosecutor
- flight attendant
- fashion model
- daycare worker

- salesperson
- C.E.O.
- Web designer
- psychiatrist
- fashion designer
- accountant
- high school teacher
- gossip or advice column writer
- TV news reporter

- TV news anchor
- journalist
- TV or radio talk-show host
- translator / simultaneous interpreter
- telemarketer

2. With your classmate(s), discuss the following questions. Be prepared to explain your opinion to your classmates?

1. What are some of the good things (pros) about the job?
2. What are some of the bad things (cons) about the job?
3. What adjectives (interesting, rewarding, challenging, exhausting, etc.) would you use to describe the job?
4. What personality traits (ambitious, fair, clear-thinking, determined, hardworking, honest, patient, self-confident, calm, positive, etc.) are needed to do the job well?
5. What skills, abilities, and specific training are needed to do the job well?
6. Would you be good at the job? Could you make a successful career in it?

Mock Interview

The following is a list of some of the most commonly asked job interview questions.

A. Work with a partner and choose a few questions.

B. Working alone, take a few minutes and practice answering the questions that you and your partner have chosen. For most of the questions, you will need to provide examples and evidence to support your answers. Make sure that you know what job you are applying for.

C. Work with your partner, and take turns being an interviewer and an interviewee. Take turns asking and answering the questions.

General

- Tell me a little about yourself.
- What are you looking for in a job?

Future Goals

- What are your goals for the future?
- What are you doing to reach your goals?
- Describe a goal that you have already accomplished. How did you accomplish it?
- Where do you want to be five years from now? Ten years from now?

School and Work History

- How has your education or past work experience prepared you for the job that you are applying for?
- What do you classmates/co-workers say about you?

Your Qualities and Characteristics

- Why should we hire you?
- Are you self-motivated and a self-starter?
- What are your strengths as an employee?
- Tell me about some mistakes you've made and what you did to correct them.
- Are you a team player?
- How do you make important decisions?
- What is more important to you: money or work?
- Tell me about your ability to work under pressure.
- Describe your work ethic.
- What have you learned from mistakes on the job or at school?

Discussion

You and Your Job

1. What are your priorities when looking for a job? Is receiving a high salary the most important priority, or are there other, more important considerations? Which factors are not really important to you? Explain your opinions. Here are some possibilities:

   - good working conditions
   - a boss you like
   - co-workers you like
   - little or no overtime
   - good opportunities for promotion

   - the location of the workplace
   - good opportunities for travel
   - flexible working hours
   - interesting work

2. Which of the follwing is the most attractive to you? Give reasons for your choice.
   - working for a large multinational company
   - working for a large domestically-owned company
   - working for a small- or medium-sized domestically-owned company
   - freelancing
   - owning your own company

3. Which is more important: making really good money or enjoying your job? If you had to choose between a well-paying job and a more satisfying job, which would you choose?

4. If you could choose any career, what would it be? What is your dream job? Do you think you could realistically get it?

5. Do you prefer to work alone, or as part of a team?

6. If you had to choose between a well-paying job in America and a medium-paying job in your home country, which would you choose? Under what kind of circumstances would you move to a foreign country for work?

7. If you could own your own business, what would it be? Do you have any long-term plans to start a new business? What obstacles do you think you would face?

8. Do you want to obtain any additional training to prepare yourself better for employment or get a promotion? Do you want to earn an MBA? Where would you like to go to earn it?

9. What do you think would be the most interesting job?

10. What job do you want to have in five years' time? In ten years' time?

11. What three adjectives would you use to describe yourself as a worker?

12. When you were a child, what did you want to be when you grew up?

13. Do you consider yourself to be an ambitious person at work? Would you describe yourself as a workaholic?

14. Do you feel that your education has prepared (is preparing) you well for your job/career?

15. If you are a man, would you be bothered if your wife made more money than you? Would you ever be willing to become a househusband?

16. If you have a job, are you satisfied with it?

17. Among the people you know, who has the best job or career? Who among the people you know has the most interesting job? What is it?

18. If you are a student, what kind of job do you hope to find after graduation? What special skills do you have to offer an employer?

19. If you have a job, would you want your children to do your job?

The Job Search and Hiring Process

1. What are some questions that are frequently asked in a job interview?

2. If you were in charge of hiring people for a company, what questions would you ask in an interview? Are there any questions that are never asked in an interview that should be asked?

3. You have to hire a new employee for your firm. Two people have applied; you must choose one. Candidate A has ten years of experience and an excellent track record at a company very similar to yours, but he has only a high school education. Candidate B is a recent university graduate and has a degree in a field closely related to your company's business. Who would you choose?

4. Many candidates "embellish" the truth, write "half-truths," and, in some cases, write outright lies on their resumes. What do you think of candidates who do this? Given the difficult economy, is it acceptable? Would you do the same thing?

5. What special job-related skills or personal qualities should a university candidate have these days if he/she hopes to be successful in landing a job?

6. What is the hardest question you've ever had to answer in a job interview?

7. Have you ever told a lie in a job interview?

8. What are some do's and don'ts for a job interview?

9. If you have a job, was it easy for you to find your present job?

10. Do you think beauty should or should not be taken into consideration when companies choose employees? Is it morally acceptable to hire on the basis or appearance rather than ability? What desirable qualities do beautiful women and handsome men bring to the workplace?

Workplace Issues

1. What do you think of office romances?

2. What are the qualities of a good boss?

3. Some bosses ask their employees to work overtime for no extra pay. What do you think about this practice? How would you feel if it happened to you? Is it fair?

4. Most North American businesses pay employees according to the "merit principle," but in some other parts of the world businesses pay employees according to seniority. Which payment criterion is better? What are the advantages and disadvantages of each?

9 Life and Death

Language Points

a funeral service

> He died a week ago. His funeral service was held four days ago at St. Matthew's Church. The flowers and music were beautiful. All his family and friends attended.

a eulogy

> His life-long friend gave a beautiful eulogy. We were all so inspired to hear about what a wonderful life he led.

an open-casket funeral

> My mother insists that she will not have an open-casket funeral after she dies. She doesn't want people staring at her when she is dead.

creepy

> Many Halloween stories (about haunted houses, dead people, ghosts, etc.) are really creepy.

a will / to will something to someone

> According to his will, his house will be sold, and the money from the sale will be divided evenly between his three children.

queasy

> I had a terrible cruise. We met a big storm, and the huge waves made me feel queasy.

cremation / to be cremated / an urn

> He was cremated, and his ashes were kept in an urn.

a recipe for a long life

> He exercises every day, eats healthy food, and sleeps eight hours a night. He thinks that these three things are the recipe for a long life.

heredity / hereditary / inherited

> He has cancer. He has led a really healthy life, so the disease must be hereditary.

fatal

> There was a fatal accident on this road last night. Two people were killed by a speeding truck.

Dialogue

Two coworkers talk outside a funeral parlor after the funeral of their manager's wife.

Miriam: Well...that was a lovely service, wasn't it?

Gemma: For sure. Mr. Hutchinson's **eulogy** for his wife was really beautiful. I'm sure she's smiling, wherever she is now.

Miriam: Yeah. It was very fitting. Didn't she look so peaceful? The **funeral director** did a nice job with the clothes and make-up. She looked like she was just sleeping, didn't she?

Gemma: Um...well, to tell you the truth, I tried not to look. I wasn't expecting an

open-casket funeral. No disrespect to Mrs. Hutchinson, but it was really **creepy**.

Miriam: The first time I saw an open-casket funeral, I felt uncomfortable, too. Next time you won't feel so...

Gemma: No way! That was the first and last time. I really didn't like it.

Miriam: Suit yourself. [Pause]
Well, what do you want your funeral to be like?

Gemma: I don't care at all. I'll be dead, so I won't see it.

Miriam: But don't you have some preferences? You should write them down in your will. Otherwise, your family will decide, and it might not be what you wanted.

Gemma: I guess so. I just want it to be **inoffensive**...something that won't make people feel **queasy**. What's yours going to be like?

Miriam: I want to have an open-casket service, just like Mrs. Hutchinson - I thought it was really nice to see her like that, one last time - and then I think I'll be cremated. I want my ashes to be put up at my parent's cottage in the Adirondacks.

Gemma: Hmm. Well, I'd better get going. I'll see you on Monday.

Comprehension

1. Briefly explain what the two women are talking about.

2. What was Gemma's reaction to the funeral service?

3. What was Miriam's reaction to it?

4. Why did Gemma suddenly leave?

5. What do you think your reaction to an open-casket funeral service would be?

Activity A

Calculate Your Life Expectancy

How long would you like to live? Do you want to live to a ripe old age, or would you rather live fast and die young. There is an old saying that claims that "there are only two certainties in life: death and taxes." Death seems unavoidable, but we can increase our chances of a long and happy life by following a few simple rules. According to statistics, the best recipe for a long life is to avoid dangerous life-shortening habits such as heavy drinking, smoking and over-eating. Heredity also plays a role especially when it comes to fatal illnesses such as heart disease and strokes. This short test will show you how long life-insurance experts expect you to live.

Work with your classmate(s) and answer YES or NO to the following:

		Yes	No	+/- 72	
1	Are you male?			−3	
2	Are you female?			+4	
3	Are you aged between 30 and 40?			+2	
4	Are you aged between 40 and 50?			+3	
5	Are you aged between 50 and 60?			+4	
6	Are you aged between over 70?			+5	
7	If you are over 65, are you still working?			+3	
8	Do you live in an urban area with a population greater than 2,000,000?			−2	
9	Do you live in a rural area with a population under 10,000?			+2	
10	Do you live alone?			−3	
11	Do you live with a partner or close friend?			+5	
12	Do you have a college or university degree?			+1	
13	Do you have a master's degree or PhD?			+2	
14	Is your income in the top 5% of the population?			−2	
15	Do you work in a mainly sedentary job?			−3	
16	Does your work involve strenuous physical activity?			+3	
17	Do you exercise at least three times a week?			+2	
18	On average, do you sleep more than 10 hours in a 24-hour period?			−4	
19	Are you happy?			+1	
20	Are you unhappy?			−2	
21	Are you quick tempered and aggressive?			−3	
22	Are you relaxed and easy-going?			+3	
23	Have you had a traffic accident in the last year?			−1	
24	Do you smoke more than 40 cigarettes a day?			−8	
25	Do you smoke 20-40 cigarettes a day?			−6	
26	Do you smoke 1-20 cigarettes a day?			−3	
27	On average, do you have 2 alcoholic drinks a day?			−1	
28	Are you more than 20 kilos overweight?			−8	
29	Are you 10-20 kilos overweight?			−4	
30	Are you 5-10 kilos overweight?			−2	
31	Do you have a physical check-up regularly?			+2	
32	Did any of your grandparents live to be over 85?			+2	
33	Did all four of your grandparents live to be over 80?			+6	
34	Did either of your parents die of a heart attack before reaching 50?			−4	
35	Did anyone in your immediate family develop cancer or a heart condition before they were 50?			−3	
	Total				

Scoring: Only YES answers count. Start with a life expectancy of 72 and then, for each question to which you answered yes, add or subtract the number of years shown in the list. Compare your results with the results of your classmate(s).

Are you satisfied with the results of this test? Ideally, how long would you like to live?

Things to Do and Places to See Before You Die

A. Work with a partner or in a small group. Read the list and choose the ten things that you most want to do before you die. Explain your choices to your partner.

- ☐ Become a millionaire
- ☐ Learn to speak English fluently
- ☐ Learn to speak another foreign language fluently
- ☐ Attend an Olympic sporting event or final
- ☐ Attend a World Cup football match
- ☐ Attend a Premier League match in England
- ☐ Be an extra in a movie
- ☐ Write a book / get a book published
- ☐ Earn a master's degree or Ph.D.
- ☐ Go skydiving
- ☐ Go skiing in the Canadian Rockies
- ☐ Go skiing in the Swiss or Austrian Alps
- ☐ Climb the Great Pyramids of Egypt
- ☐ Buy / live in a villa near a beach
- ☐ Go on an African safari
- ☐ Visit the Brazilian rainforest
- ☐ Own a luxury sports car
- ☐ Go gambling in Las Vegas
- ☐ Live in a foreign country
- ☐ Get married
- ☐ Have a great relationship with my spouse
- ☐ Have children / become a mother or father
- ☐ Learn to play a musical instrument competently

- ☐ Ride the highest roller coaster in the world
- ☐ Attend the carnival in Rio de Janeiro
- ☐ Climb up to Machu Picchu in Peru
- ☐ Go scuba diving near tropical islands
- ☐ Run a marathon
- ☐ Go bungee jumping in New Zealand
- ☐ See the Aurora Borealis / northern lights
- ☐ Make a music CD
- ☐ Spend a lot of time with my family
- ☐ Meet my first love again
- ☐ Backpack through Europe
- ☐ Travel around the world
- ☐ See all the Seven Wonders of the World
- ☐ Visit all seven continents
- ☐ Get a job that I love
- ☐ Go to Disney World
- ☐ Go on a shopping spree in New York, Paris, London or Tokyo
- ☐ Be happy and satisfied with what I have
- ☐ Raft through the Grand Canyon or see it by helicopter
- ☐ Go on a Mediterranean Cruise

B. What other things do you want to do before you die?

C. Is there anything that you have already done that everyone should do before they die?

1. If you were to die this evening, what would you most regret about your life? What would you be most proud of? If you died with no chance to communicate with anyone, what would you most regret not having told someone?

2. Would you like to know the precise date of your death? How would it change your lifestyle?

3. If you were able to live to the age of 90 and retain either the body or the mind of a 30 year old for the last 60 years of your life, which one would you choose?

4. Would you agree to be **cryogenically** frozen if you contracted a disease for which there was no cure? Do you think you would be able to adapt to society if you were **revived** and cured 100 years later?

5. Would you rather die a hero's death, die in a natural disaster, or die peacefully? Why is it so tempting to have death catch us in our sleep?

6. Do you believe in ghosts? Is it possible to communicate with the dead?

7. Some cultures feel that a funeral should be a celebration of a person's life, while other cultures feel that it should be a **sombre** occasion. What do you think? What is a typical funeral in your country like?

8. What would you most like to be remembered for? What do you think people will say about you after you pass away?

9. Do you think that the media has **desensitized** us to violence? Do you think we take death and violence lightly?

10. Is it a good idea to write a **will**? How about a **living will**?

11. Would you be willing to take medication that would miraculously double your life span? What would be the social **repercussions** of such a drug?

12. Would you consider cloning yourself (or a loved one) before dying?

13. Do you think that there is anything worth dying for? Would you die to save your country from a foreign invasion?

14. Would you give up a vital organ for your children? Your parents? Your girlfriend/boyfriend? Your husband/wife?

15. Euthanasia, the painless killing of people who are incurably ill or very old, is illegal in many western countries, including the US and the UK. However, many people approve of it in certain cases, and would like to see the laws changed. Is euthanasia legal or illegal in your country? What do you think of it?

16. If you could choose how you were going to die, what kind of death would you choose?

LESSON

10 Who Wears the Pants?

Language Points

to be equal to someone
> Jake, I've always thought that men are equal to women.

to be henpecked / a henpecked husband
> Sure, I've seen a lot of henpecked husbands, but I've also seen a lot of women being bossed around.

to have second thoughts
> These days, I'm starting to have second thoughts about it.

to give someone a hand
> I was just giving my mother a hand moving some furniture up to the attic.

a mama's boy
> My girlfriend got really mad at me and started calling me a mama's boy.

between a rock and a hard place
> It turned out that I had forgotten her birthday. I was between a rock and a hard place. I didn't have a clue what I should do.

to walk out on someone
> Janet left me in the end. Can you believe she walked out on me after 15 years of marriage?

a (social) stigma / stigmatized
> I'm a bit hesitant to get back into the dating scene. Divorcees are usually stigmatized, aren't they?

Dialogue

Two women talk about their husbands.

Jenny: Hey, you look stressed out, Maria. What's the problem?

Maria: Oh, my husband and I got into another argument again this morning. He has a terrible habit of just throwing his dirty clothes all over the house. He never picks up after himself. I'm sure he thinks he married his mother and I should continue where she left off. He **doesn't lift a finger** to do anything around the house.

Jenny: Have you tried talking to him about doing his share of the housework or picking up after himself and putting his dirty clothes into the **clothes hamper**?

Maria: Of course. I don't know how many times I've begged him to clean up after himself and to help me with the housework. He says he feels **henpecked**. I never dreamed he was so sloppy and lazy before I married him. There are even times when I have to tell him to take a shower. I'm really **having second thoughts** about our future together.

Jenny: That's terrible. My husband is just the opposite. He's **more than willing** to **give me a hand** with the housework or help to feed and bathe the children. He even cooks Sunday dinner and brings me home a bouquet of flowers once a month. And he takes us on a nice vacation every year.

Maria: It sounds like you **hit the jackpot** when you married your husband. I've been married for three years and my husband hasn't bought me flowers yet. He even forgets my birthday and our anniversary. Now he's thinking about having children. Can you imagine what it would be like if we had children?

Jenny: Have you tried talking to his family about the situation? Surely they can help.

Maria: Well, my husband is a **mama's boy**, and as far as they're concerned he **can do no wrong**. But I agree with your idea because actually he doesn't do anything at all. Oh, there is one thing he can do - he can drink every day after work with his buddies. Most nights, I don't know when he gets home because I'm usually asleep.

Jenny: Gosh, Maria, it sounds like you are stuck **between a rock and a hard place**. If you stay with him, it will be only more of the same and if you **walk out on him**, you'll have a hard time for sure. People who are divorced are usually **stigmatized**.

Maria: I think I can deal with the social stigma better than the unhappy relationship at home. At least it can't be any worse.

Comprehension

1. Can you summarize the above conversation in your own words?

2. What are Maria's biggest complaints about her husband?

3. What is Jenny's husband like?

4. What do you think Maria is considering doing to solve the problem? Do you think that this would be a good solution?

Vocabulary Focus

Fill in the blanks with the correct word or expression from the box.

stigmatized	give someone a hand
henpecked	between a rock and a hard place
mama's boy	having second thoughts
walk out on someone	

1. If you have two undesirable options when confronted with a situation you could say that you are _____.

2. Many husbands nowadays _____ with the housework.

3. In some countries, people are _____ if they are divorced.

4. Often, when couples are having serious marital problems, one of the spouse will_____ the other.

5. Even though he was married, he would call his mother and complain about all the things that went wrong in his life. He was a _____.

6. She found out that her boyfriend had a drinking problem, so she was _____ about their future marriage.

7. His wife was constantly nagging him about things. He was a _____ husband.

Debate

You will be asked to defend one of the following opinions. Before you begin, read over the supporting arguments, and choose what you will focus your argument on. Remember to listen carefully to opposing positions and respond to their points. Wherever possible, give examples and facts to back up your argument.

> **Opinion 1: Women are on their way to being equal to men.**
> - A lot of progress has been made since the 1960s.
> - Men now share in the raising of children and household responsibilities.
> - Women can be found in positions of power in business and politics.
> - The media now portrays women as having successful careers.
> - Many important laws have been passed to ensure equality in the workplace.

> **Opinion 2: Women will never be equal to men.**
> - Women still earn less than men in the workforce.
> - Women are still portrayed in a superficial way in the media.
> - The majority of positions of power are still held by men.
> - Women are not as likely to receive promotions at work because employers worry about their becoming pregnant.
> - Many working women also do most of the housework.

Activity B

Justify Your Opinion

Consider your reaction to the following generalizations about men and women. Before discussing them with your classmate(s), indicate how strongly you agree or disagree with the statements below. You will be asked to give reasons for your opinions, so think about them carefully.

> **4 - Strongly Agree**
> **3 - Agree**
> **2 - Disagree**
> **1 - Strongly Disagree**

1. Men and women think alike.

2. Guys are more flirtatious than girls.

3. Men are attracted by physical beauty; women are attracted by stability.

4. Women gossip more than men do.

5. Most guys only think about one thing: sex.

6. Men are logical; women are emotional.

7. Grown men still act like little boys.

8. It is possible for men and women to be friends, even after marriage.

9. Women are easily impressed by money.

10. Guys can never forget about their first love.

Questions for Women to Answer

1. Do you think that men in your country are different from men in other countries? Explain why or why not.

2. Do you think men should do more work around the home or do you think housework is for women? Give reasons for your opinion.

3. Do you think men expect too much from women? If so, give some examples.

4. What are some of the things a man can do at home to help his wife? (Cook, wash and iron clothes, dust, vacuum, do the dishes etc.) Do you think men could be trained to do these things just as well as women can?

5. Who do you think complains more, men or women? What sorts of things do men complain about? How about women?

6. What are the qualities of a good father, grandfather and uncle?

7. Is it possible for a man to take care of a baby as well as a woman? Why or why not?

8. Do you think that men are generally messy and lack **attention to detail**? Do men tend to overlook others' emotions more often than women? What is your general opinion of men?

9. In general, do you think there are areas where men need to improve? If so, which areas do you think need improvement? Do they lack romance, compassion, manners, listening skills, etc.?

10. What are the most important things in a single man's life? What are the most important things in a married man's life?

11. Do you think that men are too attached to their mothers? Do you know of any cases where this has caused trouble between a husband and a wife?

12. Describe your ideal man.

13. Do you agree or disagree with the proverb, "Behind every successful man is a successful woman"? What do you think it means? Is it true?

14. Do you think that men have less self-control than women? Why?

15. Is drinking alcohol necessary if a man wants to succeed at work?

Questions for Men to Answer

1. Do you think that women have a tendency to complain unnecessarily about people and things? If so, what are some things they tend to complain about the most?

2. What is your idea of a perfect woman?

3. What things are important to single women? Other than taking care of the family, what things are important to married women?

4. In some countries, women are pressured to leave their jobs when they get married. Is this the case in your country? Do you think that pressuring women to leave their jobs is discriminatory? What can be done to end this practice?

5. In general, do you think that women in your country are overworked?

6. What do you think of **affirmative action** for women? Do you think the government should force companies to hire more women in **managerial** positions? Would you mind working for a woman?

7. What are some things men can do better than women around the house?

8. What woman in the history of your country impresses you the most?

9. In many countries, women are in **combat roles** in the army and are **fighter pilots** in the air force. Do you agree with this idea?

10. What jobs should women never be allowed to do?

11. Do you know many men who are male chauvinists? Is chauvinism a problem in your country?

12. Who is the most beautiful woman in your country?

13. Do you think the women of your country are fashionable? Describe a fashionable woman that you personally know.

14. Do you think **sexual harassment** in the workplace is a problem? Do you know of any cases where sexual harassment has taken place?

11 A Match Made in Heaven

Language Points

to set someone up with someone

I hear that Brent doesn't have a girlfriend. Maybe we should try to set him up with Charlotte. She's really nice and she doesn't have a boyfriend. They would be good together.

to flirt with someone

I am so angry with my boyfriend. We went to a party, and he flirted with every girl in the room. I feel like breaking up with him.

to ask someone out (on a date)

I asked her out, and she said yes. We're going for dinner and a movie on Friday night.

the opposite sex

He's comfortable speaking with other guys, but he's always nervous speaking with members of the opposite sex.

compatible

We've only been going out for a few weeks, but I already think that we're really compatible. We like the same things, we have very similar personalities, and we have the same values.

to break up / to call it a day / to split / to split up

We're not together anymore. We've decided to call it a day.

to get married / to get hitched / to tie the knot /to say 'I do'

We love each other so much that we're going to be tying the knot in May. I hope you can come to our wedding.

Dialogue

A young man and woman are having a blind date.

Jerry: ...So, what kind of movie would you like to see tonight?

Elly: (Yawn) I don't know. I don't really watch a lot of movies.

Jerry: Really? I don't think I've ever met anyone who doesn't like movies. What don't you like about them?

Elly: (Yawn) Oh, I don't know. I just think they're sort of boring.

Jerry: Alright, alright. You don't have to **bite my head off**. I was only making polite conversation.

Elly: Well, if you don't mind, I just want to finish up my coffee and get going.

Jerry: What's wrong? Is it something I said?

Elly: I just don't think we're very **compatible**, that's all. We're so different. I don't think it's working out very well.

Jerry: What makes you think that?

Elly: You really want me to tell you?

Jerry: Sure. I like it when people are honest and direct with me.

Elly: Well, **for starters**, I don't think that going out for coffee is a very good way to impress a woman, especially on the first date. It says, "You're not worth spending money on." I could understand if you were a university student with no income, but I think that someone who's earning a decent living should be able to **splurge** on something more than coffee. I mean, it is dinnertime, you know? And I think you could have dressed up a little more. Just look at those jeans you're wearing. They're filthy!

Jerry: Do you really care about those sorts of things? I didn't think you were as **materialistic** as other women, but I guess I was wrong. Isn't it **what's on the inside that counts**? Isn't it about how you treat people?

Elly: Don't you get it? Where you take a woman and how you dress says a lot about what you think of her. You should think about that the next time you have a date. Women care about those sorts of things. Anyways, if you don't mind, I'd like to go home now.

Jerry: Okay, but I don't think the next bus comes for another ten minutes.

Comprehension

1. What happened between Elly and Jerry? Can you explain their conversation briefly in your own words?

2. In Elly's opinion, what were Jerry's biggest mistakes?

3. The situation is exaggerated, but what, if anything, do you think is true about it?

4. What does the last line imply?

Reading

Everyone is looking for love, but finding a suitable **mate** can be difficult. Luckily, many people have friends who are willing to **set them up** on blind dates in hopes of making a successful match. Dating services are another option for those looking for Mr. or Miss Right, but many people are **leery** about letting a computer decide their personal relationships. There seems to be an ongoing search for true romance, and the best way to meet your perfect love is a matter of preference.

Activity A

Love and Relationship Proverbs

Match the proverbs to the meanings. Then discuss whether you agree or disagree with the proverbs. Base your answers on your own experiences with the opposite sex, as well as the experiences of your friends and other couples.

- Absence makes the heart grow fonder.
- A good man is hard to find.
- Hell hath no fury like a woman scorned.
- Beauty is in the eye of the beholder.
- Behind every great man is an even greater woman.
- Love is blind.
- The course of true love never did run smooth.

a. No one is angrier than a woman who has been rejected in love.
b. Not being with someone increases your desire for him/her.
c. When you feel in love with somebody, you see only what's beautiful in her/him. Your feelings are so strong that you do not notice anything except what you want to see.
d. It is difficult to find a suitable male partner.
e. Men often owe their success to women who support and love them.
f. No relationship is perfect. Even people who love each other dearly have disagreements and hardships in their relationship.
g. Different people have different opinions about what make a person beautiful.

Can you think of any other proverbs about love and relationships? Discuss the meanings of the proverbs and whether you agree or disagree with them.

Activity B

Matchmaker

The following 12 people are all single and looking for that perfect someone to make their lives complete. They are counting on you to match them up successfully in relationships that will be long-lasting and fulfilling. With your classmate(s), look closely at their profiles and decide what combinations you think would make the best couples.

The Ladies

Name: Erin
Age: 26
Occupation: Flight Attendant
Education: B.A. English
Personality: humorous, flirtatious, and talkative
Dating History: Has dated many guys in various countries, most of the relationships were not serious though. She is currently looking to settle down with Mr. Right.
General Information: Because of her job, she is rarely home. She lives with her parents when she is not traveling.

Name: Gina
Age: 29
Occupation: Recently lost her job as a newspaper journalist because of her controversial opinions. Now unemployed.
Education: Degree in Journalism
Personality: outspoken, opinionated, and persistent
Dating History: Has not had a boyfriend for the past four years. Prior to that, she was in a three-year relationship with her university sweetheart.
General Information: She owns her own house. She loves shopping and spending money, so she is looking for a guy who has a good job.

Name: Heather

Age: 23

Occupation: Student

Education: Currently studying Law at New York University

Personality: shy, kind, generous, and understanding

Dating History: She has never had a boyfriend, but dreams of having a romantic wedding. She has had trouble finding a boyfriend in the past because she is quite **homely**.

General Information: She is the only child of wealthy parents.

Name: Yasmin

Age: 31

Occupation: Clothing Store Owner

Education: Business Degree – Wharton School of Business

Personality: organized, sociable, moody, and stubborn

Dating History: Dated one of her professors all through college. Likes older men. Often goes on dates with married men.

General Information: She likes dancing and drinking. She lives in an apartment with her two dogs.

Name: Stephanie

Age: 24

Occupation: English Teacher

Education: Philosophy Degree - Harvard

Personality: free-spirited, idealistic, and easy-going

Dating History: Broke up with her boyfriend last year. He still loves her and wants her to come back to him.

General Information: Stephanie dreams of getting married and opening a tea room and aromatherapy shop.

Name: Minny

Age: 25

Occupation: TV personality

Education: High school

Personality: funny, stylish, and a big spender

History: Her boyfriends are constantly hounded by the media, so her relationships don't last long. She wants to meet a guy who is successful and can deal with the attention that she gets everywhere she goes.

General Information: She is very attractive. As a teenager, she was a popular TV star. Now she hosts her own talk show. She is one of the most recognizable people in the country.

The Gentlemen

Name: Stanley

Age: 27

Occupation: Web designer / computer programmer

Education: Computer Science - Carnegie Mellon University

Personality: quiet, creative, and a little anti-social

Dating History: Often meets women in Internet chat rooms. Has only ever had one "real" girlfriend.

General Information: He is a freelancer who works from home. He recently bought his own apartment in a nice neighborhood. He is busy, and his business is booming.

Name: Darren

Age: 32

Occupation: Accounting Clerk - International Trading Company

Education: Commerce Degree - University of Queensland

Personality: outspoken, quick-tempered, and likes sports

Dating History: A collection of unsuccessful relationships throughout his 20s, the longest of which was a six-month secret affair with a single mother.

General Information: He has been working in Korea for the past three years. He is about to be transferred back to Australia and wants to take a wife with him. He isn't picky.

Name: Victor

Age: 35

Occupation: Farmer

Education: Dropped out of Ohio State University to take over his family farm.

Personality: He describes himself as an "average guy".

Dating History: Recently broke up with a woman that he was engaged to for a year and a half.

General Information: He struggled to make ends meet when he first started farming, but now has a stable income. He is a hard worker and makes an average income.

Name: Jason

Age: 30

Occupation: Musician

Education: High school. Spent most of his childhood playing the guitar and performing.

Personality: happy-go-lucky, even-tempered, funny, and understanding

Dating History: His rugged good looks make him popular with the ladies. He has had a girlfriend for five years, but doesn't want to marry her, and often cheats on her.

General Information: He is spending all of his savings on recording a new CD. If it is successful, he will reap all the benefits of success. If it fails, he will lose everything.

Name: Jeremy

Age: 28

Occupation: Looking for a job. He wants to work for a multinational company.

Education: Human Resource Management Certificate - Community College

Personality: charming, lovable, and exciting

Dating History: Lived with his girlfriend for over a year. He planned to get married to her, but she broke up with him.

General Information: He has traveled all over the world. Even though he didn't do well in school, he is very clever.

Name: Kevin

Age: 24

Occupation: Stockbroker

Education: A kid-genius who earned a Master's degree in Finance when he was 21.

Personality: smart, a little strange, and a mama's boy

Dating History: Never had a girlfriend

General Information: Wants to get married as soon as possible to give himself a more stable and credible image in the finance industry.

Activity C

Dating Preferences

Whenever you use matchmaking or dating services, it's common to fill in a questionnaire about your preferences and tastes with regard to dating. Work with your classmate(s) and give each other a short interview using the questionnaire below as a guide. Remember to ask follow-up questions to find out more about what you like and dislike about dating.

1 Most of my friends would say I have a _____ personality.

a. dominant   b. easy-going
c. shy   d. other

2 I _____ the bar scene.

a. like
b. dislike

3 I prefer _____ when I go out on dates.

a. to party a lot
b. not to party

4 On a date, I tend to like lively surroundings with lots of _____.

a. talking
b. dancing
c. partying

5 I'm _____ experienced in relationships.

a. very
b. not very

6 I have had ___#___ long-term relationships.

7 Some of my favorite activities / restaurants / places to go are...

8 I like being with _____ when I'm getting to know someone.

a. one person
b. a group of people

9 Where I live is _____ important. I _____ willing to travel or move for the right person.

a. very   a. am
b. not very   b. am not

10 I'm looking for someone who wants to _____ in developing a relationship.

a. take it slow
b. waste no time

11 I like going out on dates, but my real reason for dating these days is to find a serious _____, and I'm looking for someone with the same goal.

a. long-term relationship
b. marriage partner

12 When it comes to physical health, I exercise _____, and expect my potential mates to be at about the same fitness level.

a. several times a week
b. a few times per week
c. never

13 I like the people I date to _____ .
a. be assertive in making decisions
b. follow my lead

14 My feelings on children are...

Dream Date

Take a few minutes to fill in the following questionnaire describing what you'd consider to be your dream date. Take turns giving short presentations to your classmate(s). Ask each other follow-up questions to find out more about each other's dream date.

Who would you go on a date with?

☐ Your current partner	☐ A classmate	☐ An historical figure
☐ Your spouse	☐ A friend	☐ A celebrity
☐ An ex	☐ A co-worker	☐ Other

What would be your budget for the evening?

☐ Lavish / Extravagant	☐ Comfortable	☐ Economical
☐ Upscale & Classy	☐ Average	☐ Shoe-string

When would you go out?

☐ Morning	☐ Afternoon	☐ Evening

How long would your date last?

☐ Less than 1 hour	☐ 3 to 5 hours	☐ 7 to 10 hours
☐ 1 to 3 hours	☐ 5 to 7 hours	☐ All day

How would you get there?

Luxurious	Wacky	Run-of-the-Mill
☐ Private Jet	☐ Motorcycle	☐ Taxi, Bus, or Subway
☐ Helicopter	☐ Hot Air Balloon	☐ Car
☐ Chauffeured Luxury Car	☐ Horse-drawn Carriage	☐ Bicycle
☐ Limousine	☐ Chartered Bus	☐ On foot
☐ Other	☐ Other	☐ Other

Arranged Meeting Place

☐ Your home	☐ His / her workplace	☐ A subway station
☐ His / her home	☐ A restaurant	☐ Other

What would you do?

Luxurious	Wacky	Run-of-the-Mill
☐ Private Concert	☐ Golf	☐ Singing Room
☐ Gourmet Dinner	☐ In-line Skating	☐ Movie
☐ River Cruise	☐ Amusement Park	☐ Soju Tent
☐ Exclusive Party	☐ The Zoo	☐ Dinner
☐ Other	☐ Other	☐ Other

What would you do afterwards?

☐ Coffee	☐ A Romantic Walk	☐ Other

Discussion

Love, Dating, and Marriage

1. If you are a guy, do you feel nervous before you ask someone out on a date? How do you feel if you are rejected? If you are a girl, have you ever asked a guy out? Is it common in your country for girls to ask guys out? Do you have any friends who do (have done) it?

2. Do you **flirt** a lot? Do you know someone who **flirts** a lot? In general, who flirts more: guys or girls?

3. How long should people date before they get married?

4. What is the best age for marriage? For men? For women? At what age did you get married, or do you want to get married?

5. Describe the appearance of the person you would like to date.

6. What characteristics and qualities are important to you in a girlfriend/boyfriend?

7. What makes a good husband/wife? What things contribute to a happy, successful marriage?

8. If you had to marry either a poor man you really loved, or a rich man you did not love, which would you choose?

9. Would you marry someone ten years older than you? Ten years younger?

10. Are you a good matchmaker? How many times have you **set someone up** on a date? Are any of the couples still together?

11. Are you a good judge of character? Is your first impression of someone usually correct? What do you look for?

12. Do you think that people's criteria for dating changes over time? Has your taste in guys/girls changed at all? How have your priorities changed? What kind of person do you think you will be attracted to 20 years from now?

13. Is there such a thing as a perfect relationship?

Cohabitation

1. Do you think that couples should live together before they get married? Is it a good idea? What would be the advantages and disadvantages?

2. If a female friend of yours were contemplating moving in with her long-term boyfriend, would you support her decision? What kind of advice would you give her?

3. Would you ever consider moving in with your girlfriend/boyfriend? How about if your parents were not aware of your living arrangements? Do you think that living together would allow for a better understanding of your future spouse?

4. Do you think that living together before marriage increases the possibility of success in marriage?

5. What do you think would be the most difficult adjustment necessary for living with a member of the opposite sex?

6. Are common-law marriages popular and socially acceptable in your country? Will they ever become so?

Relationship Problems, Breaking Up, and Getting a Divorce

1. Why do so many relationships not last? Why do people break up with their partners? Who usually breaks up a relationship: the woman or the man?

2. Some scientists report that passionate love only lasts 18-30 months. After this time, the chemicals in our brains that cause the feeling of passionate love wear off. Do you agree that passionate love can last no more than 2.5 years? Or do you think that love can last forever?

3. Would you prefer being "out-of-love" in a long-term relationship, or being in love for many short-term relationships?

4. What are some problems people have when they are in love? How do people feel when a relationship ends?

5. How would you feel about marrying someone who is divorced? Would it matter to you if they had a child? Is a stigma attached to divorced people in your country?

6. Do you think marriage is necessary? Do you think that all adults should get married?

7. Do you think getting married means giving up freedom? Does marriage cause stress for a lot of people?

International Marriage

1. Would you marry someone of another nationality or race?

2. What are some advantages and disadvantages of an international marriage?

3. Do you think it is more difficult to marry someone from a different country? In what ways is it more difficult?

4. Do you know anyone who married someone from a different country? What has their experience been like? Do you know their spouse? What is your opinion of him/her?

5. How would your parents feel if you married someone from a different country?

6. Is it good for children to have parents from two different countries? Why or why not?

Dealing with Your Parents

1. Which things are important to your parents when you choose a partner? Your partner's personality? Family background? Interest in having children? Job or job prospects? Social/economic class? Physical attractiveness? Age? Academic qualifications? Nationality?

2. Would you date someone you really liked if your parents did not like him or her? Have your parents ever disapproved of any of your relationships?

3. Would you marry someone your parents did not approve of?

4. Have your parents ever tried to **set you up with someone**? What kind of person was he/she? Was he/she your type? Were the two of you compatible?

5. What would your parents think if you didn't get married?

12 Advertising and Propaganda

Language Points

to bombard

Every day we are bombarded with hundreds of ads.

mass media

Advertisers use every available form of mass media to spread their messages.

brand identity / brand image

In most cases, what sells a product is not its quality, but its brand image.

to buy into something / to be taken in by something

It is amazing how many seemingly intelligent people are taken in by advertising.

eye-catching

Certainly, many ads are eye-catching and highly creative.

to misrepresent / false advertising

However, there is no denying that most advertisers have a policy of misrepresenting the products that they are promoting.

propaganda

I believed the company's propaganda and bought their product. But now I know that their advertising is exaggerated and false.

a slogan

Nike is famous for advertising slogans, such as "Just do it!" and "Impossible is nothing."

a promotional/publicity/sales/marketing gimmick

Some gimmicks, like "buy-one-get-one-free" offers, can save you money. But other gimmicks, like the use of bright colors and stylish designs, don't save you money and don't improve the functionality of the product.

Dialogue

An ad executive is being interviewed for a radio program.

Interviewer:	Joe Montague's ad agency, M & Company, has become an industry leader in only a few short years. His ads for Xenox and Flexatela have sparked controversy, earned him industry awards, and created a new voice of conscience in the advertising industry. He speaks with us from his office in New York. [Pause] Mr. Montague, good morning. Thanks for taking the time to talk with us.
Joe:	Yes, good morning...uh...it's a pleasure.
Interviewer:	What does advertising mean to you?

Joe:	I've always thought that advertising as a medium is mostly just creative lying.
Interviewer:	[Chuckling] "Creative lying"? What do you mean?
Joe:	Well, I think that advertisers have a lot of skill and powerful tools **at their disposal**. And most of them are great at their jobs. You see some high-quality work out there. But at some point in my career, I began worrying about what we are doing in the world, what our role is - 'we' meaning advertisers. Are we just making oil companies look 'clean'? Are we just making cigarettes and alcohol look cool and fun? Are we just convincing people that they need certain things in order to be accepted? Is that how low the industry has fallen?
Interviewer:	Well, that's the whole point, isn't it? They're just trying to put the products in the best possible light. Everyone knows that. So...would you mind explaining why that's a problem for you?
Joe:	Advertising goes beyond just making things look good. The selection of products is vast, but they are essentially all the same. In most cases, **brand identity** is the only real **distinction**. The competitive advantage is brand name, not product **attributes**. And think about it...what is brand identity, really? It's just a kind of illusion. I mean, there's nothing inherently cool or sexy about smoking or drinking. And nobody's going to become rich or good-looking simply **by virtue of** wearing a given brand of clothing. It's just this glossy, airbrushed illusion that people **buy into**.
Interviewer:	So,...what you're saying is that advertisers are tricking people into thinking that a given product is significantly different?
Joe:	Yeah, basically.
Interviewer:	Then, what was the **impetus** behind your work with Flexatela? I remember those images so clearly; the white baby being breast-fed by a black woman; that was genius...unforgettable.
Joe:	The people at Flexatela were familiar with my work and gave me a lot of leeway to do what I wanted. Their strategy was to get the maximum **press** possible. Doing that involved using shock value to catch people's attention...**jolting** them with something a little different...giving them something to think about. When people saw the ads, the idea was to create a link between those **provocative** images and the brand. We wanted people to think of Flexatela as the corporation with a social conscience.
Interviewer:	But didn't the management go insane?
Joe:	Oh, for sure. There were huge battles going on all the time. Here we were, putting out this new **genre** of ads with these shocking images, and people at Flexatela were wondering how this could possibly help them to sell more sweaters. But Luciano, the CEO, who shared my vision, would say to them, "Shut the hell up. We're doing something important here."
Interviewer:	Well, I think the campaign has done well. It has really made Flexatela into **a household name**.
Joe:	Yes, we've been quite pleased with the response.
Interviewer:	Mr. Montague, sorry but that's all we have time for today. Thanks.
Joe:	You're welcome.

1. Who is Joe Montague?

2. Does the description of his ad campaign remind you of any ads?

3. Do you think he has a positive or negative opinion about the advertising industry? Do you agree with him?

4. Do we buy things after carefully evaluating our options, or are we being subconsciously persuaded by advertising to buy one thing over another? How much control do advertisers really have over us?

5. Are there any ads that you have seen recently that you thought were obviously lying to you?

6. Sometimes the lies that advertisers tell are non-verbal. Can you think of some examples of non-verbal lies that are commonly communicated by ads?

7. One study reports that during an average day, we are bombarded with over five hundred advertisements by various media. Do you think there is too much advertising around us? Does it bother you?

Activity A

Famous Brand Names

What famous brand names do we most often associate with these common items? In these cases, the brand name has become synonymous with the product name!

- Cola

- Tissue

- Cellophane tape

- Aspartame

- Acetaminophen

- MP3 players

- Inline skates

- Photocopiers

- Bath/hot tub

- Window cleaner

- Artificial playing turf

- Lip balm

- Large trash receptacles

- Flying discs

Discuss:
Why do you think these companies / products have become **household names**?
What sort of image have they developed?

Analyze Ads

Look at the following advertisements taken from American newspapers and magazines from the 1940s. What do you think of them? What tricks are being used to convince you to buy the products? Are similar 'tricks' still used today?

Awaken love with the lure men can't resist…exotic, tempting IRRESISTIBLE PERFUME. It stirs the senses…thrills…sets hearts on fire. Use Irresistible Perfume and know the mad joy of being utterly irresistible. Men will crowd around you paying you compliments…begging for dates. Your friends will envy your strange new power to win love.

Not Just a Promise!…but actual proof from 36 leading skincare specialists that Palmolive Soap facials bring new beauty to the complexions of 2 out of 3 women…no matter what their age or skin type! Never before these tests has there been proof of such sensational beauty results. Palmolive facials really work to give you a more radiant complexion!

We only have one aim in mind when we plan our services for your journies with TWA: When you reach your destination feeling so refreshed and relaxed, you will think it's a shame to come down to earth. Then you've really had a taste of airline travel the way TWA people strive to make it.

Famous Advertising Slogans

Work with a partner. The following are 12 of the most famous and successful slogans in the history of U.S. advertising. Match the slogan to the company that created it.

1. "Don't leave home without it."
2. "The ultimate driving machine."
3. "A diamond is forever."
4. "Put a tiger in your tank."
5. "Good to the last drop."
6. "Does she… or doesn't she?"
7. "Think small."
8. "The skin you love to touch."
9. "Look, Ma! No cavities!"
10. "Takes a licking and keeps on ticking."
11. "Look sharp, feel sharp."
12. "You'll wonder where the yellow went."

a. Clairol hair color
b. Gillette razors
c. Pepsodent toothpaste
d. Volkswagen
e. Woodbury Soap
f. American Express credit cards
g. Esso oil/gasoline
h. Times watch company
i. Maxwell House coffee
j. Crest toothpaste
k. BMW
l. DeBeers mining company

Discuss the slogans with your partner(s). What key benefit of the product does each slogan refer to? Why do you think it was a successful slogan? Would it work in your country?
What are some of your favorite advertising slogans, and why do you like them?

Design an Ad

With your group, choose a product to design an advertising strategy for. You can pick an existing product or you can invent one of your own! Follow these guidelines to help you prepare your plan.

1. Choose a product or company to represent.

2. Define the target market (age, gender, income)

3. Discuss the advantages of the various kinds of media to advertise your products, and decide where the ad should be placed: on TV, in newspapers, on the radio, on billboards, on milk cartons, in public washrooms, on leaflets handed out on the street, on the internet, at sporting events, etc.

4. Create a catchy slogan for your product. Your slogan should be memorable, refer to a key benefit of the product, and help customers instantly recognize the brand.

5. Think of an ideal spokesperson (possibly a celebrity) for the product.

6. Decide on a style of ad (controversial, touching, funny, informative, inspiring, shocking, sexy, etc.)

7. Come up with a gimmick (attractive colors, packaging, pictures, cartoons, or other eye-catching features; free gifts; buy one, get one free offers; etc.) to ensure that this product gets everyone's attention.

8. Explain why your product is superior to your competitor's product (range of functions/features, workmanship/durability/reliability, design/style/appearance/taste, ease of use/simplicity, comfort, health/safety, price/cost, etc.)

After you have worked out the details, present your ideas to the rest of the class. Feel free to give feedback to your classmates about their ideas. Would their advertising plans convince you to buy their products? Why or why not?

1. What companies are most "in your face" in your country?

2. To what extent do you think advertising affects your spending habits and daily life? Are some people brainwashed by the media?

3. Is it true that **there is no such thing as bad press**? What examples are there of bad publicity having a favorable result?

4. Which stars, celebrities and athletes do you think receive too much media hype?

5. Can overexposure sometimes cause consumers and fans to get sick and tired of their favorite stars?

6. What are your favorite ads? Are the products advertised by these ads also products that you buy frequently?

7. What are the most annoying commercials on TV?

8. Are there any celebrities that you feel are "**sell outs**"?

9. What are the most important factors when you make your purchases? Do you ever buy things because they are popular? Inexpensive? Expensive? Foreign? Domestically produced? Unique?

10. Which brands do you prefer when buying / frequenting the following? Why do you like them?

Shoes	Fast food
Coffee	Cola
Clothes	Handbags / Book bags
Cell Phones	Beer / Alcoholic beverages
Cars	Coffee shops

11. How much of youth culture is made by youths themselves, for themselves, and how much is marketed and sold to them by corporations?

12. Reflect on the following quote, using evidence from your experience: "One of the effects of branding is to make you feel as if you are part of a community." (Phil Knight, CEO, Nike Corporation)

13. Are some sources of information more reliable than others? Where do you get your news? Which sources do you not trust?

14. Are you loyal to any brands? Which international brands? Which domestic brands? Why do you prefer these brands over others?

15. Are some people more brand-conscious than others? Why are they like that? Are you brand-conscious?

16. Have you ever bought imitation branded clothing?

17. Have you (or anyone you know) ever been a victim of **false advertising**? Does it happen to you often?

13 Superstitions, Mysteries and the Paranormal

Language Points

a superstition / superstitious

There's an old superstition that killing a spider brings you bad luck, and when I was a child, I was superstitious, so I never killed any spiders.

paranormal

I don't believe in anything paranormal. If there is no scientific explanation, I don't believe it.

a conspiracy / a conspiracy theory

He joined the conspiracy to overthrow the government.

a coincidence

You're flying to London next week? What a coincidence! So am I!

a premonition

I had a premonition that my life was about to change for the worse. Then I had a car accident, and my girlfriend broke up with me.

telepathy / telepathic

Sometimes my girlfriend knows exactly what I am thinking. Sometimes I think that she must be telepathic.

a hoax

The UFO sightings were revealed to be a hoax, just like the Loch Ness Monster.

Dialogue

Scott rushes over to Aaron's house after receiving a desperate phone call.

Scott: Aaron, what's up? You look **as pale as a ghost**. Is there anything wrong?

Aaron: Yes, as I mentioned to you the other day, I have an important job interview today but I'm afraid to leave the house.

Scott: I remember you **talked endlessly** about your job interview with the brewery. You're a **shoe-in** for that job. Why are you afraid to leave the house?

Aaron: Last night, when I was coming home, a black cat crossed my path, and this morning, I accidentally broke my living room mirror when I was rearranging the furniture.

Scott: Aaron, you're not superstitious, are you? You have to go to that interview.

Aaron: Scott! What day is today?

Scott: Why, it's Friday the 13th. But Aaron, aren't you **going a little overboard**? Don't you think these are all **coincidences**?

Aaron: **What's even worse** is that my interview is on the 13th floor.

Scott: Aaron, you sound **paranoid**. I think you're **making a mountain out of a molehill**. But if it'll help, I'll loan you my lucky rabbit's foot. It has been a **lucky charm** for me in the past. Just rub it when you feel anxious.

Aaron: Will it really work?

Scott: No question. It works for me. I used it when I got my accounting job. Besides, I'll **have my fingers crossed** for you.

Aaron: You know, Scott, I heard a magpie singing this morning. Maybe things aren't as bad as they seem. You're a real pal. I'll go and put on my new suit for the interview.

Scott: Good luck!

Comprehension

1. Why is Aaron still at home when he has an important job interview?

2. How does Scott convince Aaron that things aren't so bad?

3. How many examples of different superstitions can you find in the dialogue?

Activity A

Strange Events

Match the words below with the situations (1-8)

an unsolved murder	a ghost story
a conspiracy theory	a premonition
a mysterious disappearance	telepathy
a coincidence	a hoax

1. In 44 BC, Calpurnia Pisonis Julius, Caesar's wife, had a dream the night before her husband died that he would get stabbed by a friend, and she warned him not to go to the Roman Senate, where he was killed.

2. Two American presidents, John Adams (president, 1796-1800) and Thomas Jefferson (president, 1800-1808), died on exactly the same day. And it was not just any day, but July 4, 1826, the fiftieth anniversary of the Declaration of Independence.

3. On October 30, 1938, a series of radio news bulletins announced that the world was being attacked by invaders from Mars. Many listeners were terrified and began to panic. Some fled their homes.

4. An entire squadron of 5 US military aircraft and their crews disappeared while flying a routine training mission off the coast of Florida on December 5, 1945. The Navy and the US government launched an enormous air search totaling 4,100

hours and covering 380,000 square miles. No wreckage was ever found from any of the planes.

5. In Charles Dickens' 1843 novel *A Christmas Carol*, Ebenezer Scrooge is visited by four spirits on Christmas Eve. They show him how he has misused his life, and their influence changes him.

6. Without warning, a healthy man felt a suffocating pain in his chest. Hundreds of miles away at the same moment, his identical twin suffered a heart attack.

7. In 2006, a wealthy Canadian businessman and his wife were stabbed to death in their room at a luxury resort in Cancun, Mexico, where they were attending their daughter's wedding ceremony. No motive has ever been established, and no suspects have been arrested.

8. US President Kennedy was assassinated in 1963. The exact motive for his killing, and the identity of his killer, have never been established. Many people reject the government's claim that Kennedy's injuries were caused by a single gunman.

Do you know of any cases (i.e., unsolved murders, conspiracy theories, mysterious disappearances, coincidences) in your own country similar to the ones listed above? Discuss with a partner or in a small group.

Can you recall any strange or unexplained events in your life?

Activity B

Something that Happened to You

Tell your partner(s) about an important event in your life that happened by chance. It should be an event that has influenced your life in some important way.

- Was it a stroke of good luck? Something very unlucky? A serious accident? A chance meeting?

- When did it happen?

- What happened exactly?

- Why has it been important in your life?

- How did it affect your life? Did it influence you for the better, or for the worse?

- Are you happy it happened? Or do you wish it had never occurred?

- How would your life be different if it had not occurred?

Fortune Teller

You will be given the name of someone else in your class. Think about what you know about them and then try to make some predictions about their future. Use the table below to help you organize your thoughts. Give a short presentation to the class, without referring to the person by name (call them 'Person X'). The class will try to guess, from what you predict, whose fortune you are talking about.

Prediction	Time Frame
I think 'Person X' will	in (a month / a year) / on (a date) / at (a time)
❶ ❷ ❸	❶ ❷ ❸
I think that 'Person X' will be ~ing	in (a month/ a year) / on (a date) / at (a time)
❶ ❷ ❸	❶ ❷ ❸
I think that 'Person X' will have ~	by / before (a month / a year / a date / a time)
❶ ❷ ❸	❶ ❷ ❸

How Superstitious Are You?

In an age in which cold hard scientific facts are supposed to have replaced superstition, it's surprising how many people continue to consult fortune tellers and read their daily horoscopes. So, how superstitious are you? First, rate yourself on the scale below. Then, with your partner(s), answer the following questions to find out how superstitious you really are!

How superstitious do you think you are?

Not at all superstitious   Very superstitious

1——2——3——4——5——6——7——8——9——10

	Yes	No

1. At a wedding, if the groom drops the wedding band during the ceremony, the marriage is doomed.

2. If you break a mirror, you will have seven years of bad luck.

3. If a bee flies into your home, you will soon have a visitor. If you kill the bee, you will have bad luck or the visitor will be unpleasant. If there is a swarm of bees on your roof, your house will burn down.

4. If you blow out all the candles on your birthday cake with the first puff, you will get your wish.

5. If three people are photographed together, the one in the middle will die first.

6. If you wish on a shooting star, it will come true.

7. If you walk under a ladder, someone will have an accident.

8. If you make a wish while throwing a coin into a well or fountain, the wish will come true.

9. If two people make a wish and pull apart the dried breastbone of a chicken or turkey until it breaks, the person who gets the longer half of the wishbone will have his/her wish come true.

10. If you do not hold your breath while going past a cemetery, you will breathe in the spirit of someone who has recently died.

For each question you answered 'yes' to, score 1 point and for each one you answered 'no', score 0 points. Then total your score and rate yourself once again on the scale below.

How superstitious are you really?

Not at all superstitious   Very superstitious

1——2——3——4——5——6——7——8——9——10

Discussion

1. Are people in your country generally more superstitious than people from foreign countries?

2. What are some superstitions in your country? Do you think there is some truth behind some superstitions?

3. How many superstitions from foreign countries do you know about? Name some.

4. What superstitions did you have as a child? Do you have any superstitions now? Were you afraid of the dark when you were young? If so, what did you do?

5. Why are some people afraid to admit that they are superstitious?

6. What are some good luck (and bad luck) superstitions in your country?

7. What do you do for good luck? Do you have any lucky charms or items you carry with you on special occasions? Do you have a lucky hat / shirt / pencil for exams? Do you have a lucky number? Do you really think it brings you good luck?

8. What do you know about Nostradamus? Do you think that some people can predict the future?

9. Do you know anyone who visits a psychic regularly?

10. Have you ever been to see a fortune teller? What were you told? Did (do) you believe their predictions? Was it worth the money? If you have not been to a fortune teller, would you like to visit one?

11. What five questions would you like to ask a fortune teller? What answers would you like to hear to your questions?

12. Do you believe that there are people who have special abilities to communicate with the spirit-world and see the future and the past?

13. Do you believe in ESP? Can some people know what others are thinking or feeling?

14. Do you believe in life after death? What happens to people after they die? Do they go to Heaven? Hell?

15. Do you believe in reincarnation?

16. Do you believe your ancestors are watching you?

17. Is it possible that UFOs exist? Have you ever seen one? If you had no proof, would you tell someone you'd seen a UFO?

18. Do you know anyone who says he/she has seen a UFO? How would you respond if someone told you they'd seen one?

19. Do you know anyone who has said that they have seen a ghost? If one of your friends told you they had seen a ghost, would you believe him/her? Why/Why not?

20. If you were a ghost, who would you haunt?

21. Do you believe in miracles? Do you know of any miracles?

22. Have you (or anyone you know) ever had a dream that later came true? Have you ever had a dream that predicted the future?

23. Can you remember your dreams? Do you often have dreams? How about recurring dreams? How about nightmares?

14 Transportation

Language Points

to rear-end (the car in front of you) / to get rear-ended

> I stopped quickly, and got rear-ended. I wasn't hurt, but I have to take my car to the garage for repairs.

the jaws of life

> My uncle was in a serious car accident. His car was so badly damaged that they had to use the jaws of life to cut open his car and rescue him.

a backseat driver / to backseat drive

> My mother is a backseat driver. She is always trying to tell my father what to do when he is driving. He gets really impatient with her.

to be caught in traffic

> I'm going to be late because I'm caught in traffic. I've hardly moved for ten minutes.

a fender bender

> There was an accident, but it was really minor – only a fender bender.

to cut in / cut in front of (someone)

> Did you see that car cut in front of me? He's a really dangerous driver. I'm going to stay away from him.

an alternate route

> This road's slow. Let's find an alternate route.

a designated driver

> I'm not drinking tonight because I'm the designated driver.

traffic congestion

> There's a lot of congestion on the roads, so I might be a little late.

Dialogue

A man is driving his friend to the airport.

Yannick: I didn't think the traffic would be so heavy at this time of day. It's usually fairly light in the early afternoon.

Harry: Did you forget about all the construction in this area?

Yannick: I guess I did. I don't know what I was thinking. I certainly didn't plan on **being caught in all this traffic** for this long.

Harry: Do you know a short cut we can take to get out of this mess?

Yannick: I could make a **u-turn** and go back to the last intersection and take an **alternate route** from there.

Harry: Well, let's do it. I've only got forty-five minutes before I have to check in at the airport... Hold on. Just wait for the white van... Alright, you can go now. It's all clear.

Yannick: Ahh! That was close; you just about got us killed! I thought you said it was all clear!

Harry: It was, except for the transport truck. I thought you saw him coming. How could you have missed seeing a transport truck?

Yannick: If he had hit us, we would have been killed! They would have had to use the **jaws of life** to get our bodies out of the car.

Harry: Don't worry about what could have happened. Just get me to the airport on time. Can't you drive a little faster? You're only going 90.

Yannick: Only 90! This is a 50 zone. What do you want me to do, fly?

Harry: Watch out! That taxi just **cut in front of** us. Why didn't he signal?

Yannick: [SCREECH] Whew! That was close. I think I'll slow down just to be safe.

Harry: You drive like an old woman. Why don't you drive a little more aggressively?

Yannick: I wish you weren't such a **backseat driver**. [CRASH]

Harry: Now, look at what you've done. You've **rear-ended** that taxi. You'll have to stop and exchange information even if it is only a **fender bender**. I can't wait. I'm going to take that taxi over there. Bye, talk to you when I get back.

Yannick: What?!

Comprehension

1. In your own words, describe what happened.

2. Did they anticipate the traffic congestion? Why not?

3. Explain what is meant by the phrase "backseat driver".

4. Why is Yannick so shocked at the end of the dialogue?

Vocabulary Focus

Fill in the blanks with the correct words or expressions from the box.

caught	u-turn	alternate route
jaws of life	designated	backseat driver
cut in	rear-ended	fender bender

1. It is wise to appoint a _____ driver if you and your co-workers are planning to go out drinking for the evening.

2. I was waiting in line at the bank when a little old lady _____ ahead of me.

3. Whenever my mother-in-law is in the car she acts like a _____ and tells me what I'm doing wrong.

4. It's not unusual to get _____ in traffic during rush hour.

5. The car behind me _____ me while I was waiting at the traffic lights.

6. In serious car accidents, it is sometimes necessary to use the _____ to extract injured people from their vehicle.

7. On his way to work this morning, he was involved in a minor accident. It was a _____.

8. Sometimes, to avoid being caught up in a traffic jam, it is better to use an _____.

9. He drove too far so he made a _____ and went back the same way he came.

Activity A

What Do You Think of the Transportation System?

A. How would you rate the transportation system in Seoul? Work with a partner (or in a small group) and rate each item on a scale from 1-5. As you come up with your ratings, consider the questions.

1. excellent	2. good	3. adequate/OK
4. needs improvement	5. terrible	

KTX trains

- Do they run on time?
- Are travel times to other cities reasonable?
- Are there enough trains?
- Is the price reasonable?
- What about the quality and price of food and other services on the train?

the bus system

- Are the buses clean?
- Do they run on time? Often enough? Do they run late enough at night?
- Is the bus service fast enough?
- Are there enough bus routes?
- Are drivers polite, courteous, and helpful?
- Do they drive safely?

Seoul Station (KTX)

- Is the station modern and clean?
- How about shopping and eating possibilities?
- Is the waiting area comfortable?
- Can you buy your ticket quickly?
- Are connections to the subway convenient?

taxi services

- Are the drivers polite?
- Are the drivers knowledgeable, and can they take you exactly where you want to go?
- Do they drive safely?
- Are taxis too expensive or reasonably priced?
- Do they overcharge sometimes?

subway trains

- Are the trains fast?
- Are they reliable? Do they break down often? Are there many delays?
- Do they run on time?
- Are there enough subway lines?
- Are the subway trains crowded?
- Are they safe? Are they clean?
- Do they run late enough at night?

conditions on the roads

- Are there enough roads for the volume of traffic?
- Are there enough lanes for cars?
- Are traffic rules respected?
- Are drivers courteous and polite? Is there too much honking?
- Are there many cases of road rage?
- Are there too many accidents?

subway stations

- Are the platforms safe?
- Are they clean?
- Are there enough exits?
- Are there enough escalators?

public parking

- Are there enough public parking garages? Do garages charge fair prices for parking?
- Are there enough parking spaces on the street?
- Does it take too long to find a parking space

B. **Explain your ratings to the class.**

C. **Work with a partner or in a small group. Write five suggestions to solve the transportation problems in Seoul.**

> i.e., Bus drivers should be required to drive more safely.
> Dangerous bus drivers should be given steep fines.
> There should be more subway trains running at rush hour.

D. **Explain your suggestions to the class. The class should then decide which suggestions are the best.**

The Flight Home

A. **Discuss with your partner the meaning of each phrase.**

- a boarding announcement
- the check-in counter
- a boarding gate
- a boarding pass
- to board the plane
- to clear customs
- the overhead storage bin
- a conveyor belt
- the luggage carousel
- security clearance
- fasten your seatbelt
- the immigration counter

B. **Read each step (a-l). Write whether each step occurs in the "pre-flight," "on-board," or "post-flight" stage of air travel. Check your answers with a partner. (Hint: There are four steps for each stage.)**

a. *pre-flight* _____ Listen for the **boarding announcement**, then get in line and **board the plane**.

b. _____ Wait for the plane to stop moving, then take your baggage and head for the exits.

c. _____ Go to the **luggage carousel** and pick up your luggage.

d. _____ Arrive at the airport at least a couple hours early. Load your luggage into a luggage cart, then go to the right **check-in counter** and wait in line.

e. _____ Be sure that you have all of your luggage, and **clear customs**. Now you're ready to go home or to your hotel!

f. _____ Pass through **security clearance**, then walk to the right **boarding gate** and wait for the boarding announcement.

g. _____ Listen to the presentation on flight safety. Notice where the emergency exits are.

h. _____ Present your passport to the immigration officer to examine. Answer some questions and have your passport stamped.

i. _____ Find your seat and place your luggage in the **overhead storage bin**. Then sit down, **fasten your seatbelt** and prepare for take-off.

j. _____ Check in, get your **boarding pass**, and place the baggage you wish to be checked on the **conveyer belt**.

k. _____ Proceed with your luggage to the **immigration counter** and stand in line.

l. _____ Buckle up and prepare for landing.

C. **Put the steps in the proper sequence. Number the steps 1-12. Check your answers with a partner.**

Discussion

Air Travel

1. Have you traveled abroad? What airlines have you flown? Which airline was the best? Which airline was the worst? Which airline provided the best service? The worst service? What airline would you suggest to your partners? Which airline would you not recommend? Why?

2. Have you ever missed (or almost missed) a flight? Explain what happened?

3. How old were you when you went on your first flight? Where did you go?

4. What has been the longest flight you have ever taken?

5. What kind of seat do you prefer: window, center or aisle? Why?

6. What do you like to do during the flight? Are you able to sleep during the flight? Do airlines provide anything interesting to help pass the time? How could in-flight entertainment services be improved?

7. Do you like to buy duty-free items on the airplane or in the airport? What have you bought?

8. Have you ever seen a female pilot? Why do you think that most pilots are men? Would you like to be a pilot?

9. Would you like to be a flight attendant? What are the benefits and drawbacks or being a flight attendant?

10. What do you think should be the most important qualifications for becoming a flight attendant? Is beauty and youthfulness given too much weight in the hiring of flight attendants?

Cars

1. Do you know anyone who is a backseat driver? When your father drives, does your mother backseat drive?

2. What is road rage? Have you ever witnessed an incidence of road rage?

3. Have you ever driven in any other countries? How did it compare to driving in Korea? Do you feel that driving in Korea is more, or less, dangerous than driving in other countries? Why?

4. What is the most scenic drive in Korea? Have you ever been on a scenic drive in a foreign country? Where?

5. Have you ever been in a minor traffic accident? Whose fault was it? Have you ever been in a serious traffic accident? Do you know of anyone who has? What happened?

6. Who do you think are better drivers: men or women? (Just because there are fewer women drivers, it doesn't mean they are worse drivers than men.) Who is better at parking a car: men or women? How can you explain any differences in driving skill and parking skill between the sexes?

7. North Americans can obtain a driver's license when they turn 16. Do you think this is a good idea? If you feel that 16 is too young, what would you consider an appropriate age?

8. Do you know anyone who has driven while drunk? Do you know anyone who has been caught by the police driving while under the influence? What happened? Have you ever ridden with a drunk driver? Have you ever been the designated driver?

9. What is your favorite Korean car? Sonata? Genesis? Sportage? Santa Fe? Sorenato? Matiz? Chairman? Tico? Why?

10. Would you be embarrassed to drive a Tico? What do you think of Ticos?

11. What do/will you consider when buying a new car? (Price, color, fuel efficiency, reliability, resale price, safety, status, power, performance, etc.)

12. Would you ever consider buying a foreign car? What is your favorite foreign car?

13. If you won an expensive car like an Equus in a contest, would you keep it or sell it?

14. If you were driving and you accidentally bumped into a parked car and nobody saw it, would you leave your name and number, or would you drive away?

15. Have you ever received a traffic ticket? What had you done wrong? How much was the ticket? Have you ever received a speeding ticket? Have you received more than one? Do you know someone who has received many speeding tickets?

16. Have you ever failed a driving test? Why did you fail? What happened?

17. If you could have any kind of car, what would it be? What color would it be? Does your taste/preference in cars say anything about your personality and values?

18. What are the advantages of driving a foreign car? Why do people drive foreign cars? Is it because the quality is higher? Is it for social status and attention?

19. Do you always wear a seat belt? Even if you are in the back seat? How about on a bus?

20. What are the most annoying bad driving habits of other drivers? What things annoy you about the way other people drive?

21. Do some people's personalities change when they are behind the wheel? Do some people become less courteous, more aggressive and more impolite when they are driving? Why?

Public Transportation (Buses and Subways)

1. How do you get to English class every day? How long does it take to get here from your home? What subway lines and bus numbers do you take? Where do you have to transfer? How long does it take? How do you usually get to university or work?

2. Who are better bus drivers: Men or women? Who do you trust more?

3. When traveling long distances in Korea, do you prefer to travel by car, train, or bus? What about for traveling in Seoul: car, bus or subway? Which is more convenient? Is there a bus stop or subway station near your home?

4. Have you ever used the public transportation system in a foreign country? How was it similar to the system here? How was it different? Which was better? Which was more widely used?

5. There are women-only subway cars in a number of cities around the world, including Tokyo, Osaka, Cairo, Mexico City and Taipei. There is also a proposal to introduce women-only subway cars in Seoul in 2008. Do you support the proposal? Why or why not? Can the women-only rule be enforced?

6. Do you often sleep on the subway? Have you ever fallen asleep and missed the subway station you were going to? Why were you going there? How much time did you waste?

7. Have you ever forgotten or lost something valuable on a bus or subway? Did you get it back?

15 One More for the Road

Language Points

to have / get a buzz

> I get a buzz off just a couple of drinks.

a round (of drinks)

> Bartender, how about a round of drinks for all my good friends here?

to mix one's drinks

> You'll regret it in the morning if you mix your drinks.

to be on the wagon

> We'd better not invite John to the bar with us. He's on the wagon.

to puke / to throw up

> We can't go there! Last time I went there, I puked all over the place.

to be drunk / plastered / blasted / wasted

> Oh, my head. I was so wasted last night.

to hammer something back

> I stopped by the bar after work and hammered back half a dozen beers.

tolerance for alcohol

> If his tolerance weren't so high, he wouldn't spend so much on drinking.

to black out

> I must have blacked out. I don't remember doing any of that!

to crash

> I came home drunk, crashed on my sofa, and didn't wake up until 10:30 the next morning.

Alcoholics Anonymous (AA)

> Many recovering alcoholics belong to Alcoholics Anonymous. They go to AA meetings every week to share their experiences of recovery with other members.

bloodshot

> Drinking too much alcohol can cause your eyes to become bloodshot.

Dialogue

Two office workers talk about the night before.

Dean: Wow, Kevin, you're as white as a ghost, and your eyes are really **bloodshot**. What happened to you? Are you sick?

Kevin: I really **don't feel so hot**. I was out with Shawn until very early this morning. Boy, did we **hammer them back**! I think I'm going to be sick again. I've already **puked** three times this morning.

Dean: Where did you guys go?

Kevin: We went to that new pub around the corner. Shawn invited a couple of **chicks** over to our table and we drank with them until midnight. After the girls left, a couple of Shawn's friends came in and bought us a few more **rounds**. I really **mixed my drinks** and **got plastered**.

Dean:	Well, it's a good thing you **got home in one piece**.
Kevin:	I must have **blacked out**. I don't remember anything that happened after the girls left. I got home somehow. I **crashed** on my sofa in my clothes. What's worse, I lost my wallet and one shoe, and I somehow managed to tear the collar of my new jacket! I even lost the girls' telephone numbers. They were real fine, too.
Dean:	What a **horror show**! Your **tolerance** must be really low.
Kevin:	I'll say! I'm going **on the wagon** before my liver shuts down.
Dean:	Yeah, yeah, I've heard it all before. You say that every time you go out and **get blasted**. It's the same old story.
Kevin:	No, I really mean it this time. Shawn and I are going to **Alcoholics Anonymous**.
Dean:	You two in AA? I'll believe it when I see it.
Kevin:	I want to be like you and Lloyd. You guys go out and have a good time, get a little **buzz**, then head home. Now, that's what I call sensible drinking.

Comprehension

1. What are Kevin and Dean talking about?

2. Describe Kevin's evening in your own words.

3. Does Dean think Kevin is serious about changing his behaviour? Find evidence in the dialogue to justify your opinion.

4. Have you ever blacked out while drinking? How many hours could you not account for? Where did you find yourself when you 'snapped out of it'?

5. What's the most embarrassing thing you've ever seen someone do while drunk?

Vocabulary Focus

Fill in the blanks with the correct expression from the box.

a buzz	a few rounds	mix your drinks	crashed
on the wagon	bloodshot	puke	
AA	plastered	hammering them back	

1. What happened to your eyes? They're totally _____.

2. He stopped drinking last month. He's been _____ever since.

3. If you _____, you'll get sick and _____.

4. Look at those guys over there. They are so _____ that they can hardly walk.

5. I was so tired yesterday I _____ on the couch after watching TV.

6. Let's go over to that new pub for _____.

7. She used to drink every night until she joined _____.

8. They've drunk a lot. They've been _____ for a couple of hours now.

9. I only had one beer, but I am already starting to get _____.

Drinking Conventions in the West

A. Have you traveled to or lived in a Western country? What similarities and differences did you notice between the drinking habits and attitudes in the country you visited and your own country?

B. Read the list of drinking habits, attitudes, and statistics on the page. How does your country compare? Does your country have the same (or comparable) habits and attitudes toward drinking? Or is your country quite different? Is any of the information surprising?

Drinking with Workers and the Boss

- Western workers are never pressured to join their manager for a night of heavy drinking.
- Western workers sometimes go out "for a cold one" after work on Friday nights. Participants usually go to only one place for the whole evening and take turns buying rounds. Participants are expected to hold their liquor well and not become totally drunk.

Drinking and Food

- Westerners sometimes nibble on finger foods such as peanuts, pretzels or chips when they drink. However, eating cake or candy while drinking is unheard of in the West
- It is common for Westerners to drink wine when they have a big meal.

Drinking on Holidays and Special Occasions

- It is quite common for Western workers to share a bottle of wine on special occasions, such as Christmas. This is often done at an office party.
- Many Westerners celebrate Christmas or New Year's with a drink of eggnog — consisting of sweetened milk or cream, eggs and alcohol, usually rum or brandy.
- During a wedding, free drinks are often served to guests during the reception, known as "an open bar."

Drinking in Restaurants and Pubs

- Good news is often celebrated by having a few drinks in a pub.
- Buying someone a drink is a gesture of goodwill, and can be used to express thanks or to mark the resolution of a dispute.
- To indicate interest and initiate conversation (or at least flirtation), it is common for a person to buy a member of the opposite sex a drink at a singles bar.
- Some bars have one night a week when "ladies drink free," a ploy designed to bring more female visitors to a bar and thereby bring in more male patrons.

Attitudes Toward Intoxication/Drunkenness

- In countries settled and influenced by British populations, drinking to a moderate level of drunkenness is generally acceptable.
- Someone lying in the street in the West is usually scooped up and taken to the drunk tank. Later, they are required to appear before a judge and usually receive a fine.
- The Scandinavian countries have strong (anti-alcohol) movements, often supported by government funds, and many people abstain from alcohol consumption.

Drinking and University Life

- Binge drinking – the rapid consumption of a large quantity of alcohol solely for the purpose of intoxication – is common among university students throughout the West, especially after final exams.
- Drinking games are common only among university students. Drinking games are rarely played after university.

Drinking and Children

- In much of Europe, but not in North America, many children and adolescents experience alcohol early, such as watered-down wine with a meal, with the approval of their parents.
- The average Canadian consumes their first alcoholic drink at just over the age of 12.

Role-play

**Work in pairs. Decide who will be 'Student A' and who will be 'Student B'.
Read through your respective instructions and act out the role-play.**

Student A

You've been at a party with some friends, but it's late and you want to go home. You came to the party by car. You've had a few drinks, but you feel alright to drive. You don't want to leave your car because you'll have to make another trip to pick it up tomorrow.

You feel confident about driving because you:
- have done it many times before
- know the way home very well
- have driven when you were much drunker than this
- are sure there aren't many cars on the streets at this time of night
- are a very good driver
- are not afraid

YOU WILL SPEAK FIRST. Tell your partner, in a slightly drunken voice, that you're tired and you feel like you'd better get going. Be stubborn about wanting to drive home.

Student B

You've been at a party having a good time. You normally drink, but tonight you decided not to because you were feeling a little sick. One of your friends has been drinking quite a lot, but you can't understand why, since you know that he/she drove to the party. Now, it's time to go and your friend is holding the car keys and is obviously planning on driving home.

You are worried that your friend:
- will certainly have an accident
- might get stopped by the police and arrested
- may injure or even kill someone
- will lose her/his driver's license
- will not be covered by insurance
- might be hurt or killed

LISTEN TO YOUR CLASSMATE, AND THEN RESPOND. You are really worried about your friend. Be stubborn about not letting her/him drive.

For Drinkers

1. Why do people drink?

2. Do people drink only to socialize or are there other reasons?

3. How often do you go out drinking?

4. When was the last time you got **blasted**?

5. Do you know anyone who is a **cheap drunk**?

6. What are some good remedies for a hangover?

7. How often do you go out **barhopping**?

8. Have you ever been harassed by a drunk?

9. When was the first time you tasted alcohol?

10. Have you ever been given a **Breathalyzer test**?

11. Have you ever tried **homebrew**?

12. Do you ever drink alone?

13. Do you have a high or low tolerance for alcohol?

14. Do you ever feel like you are drinking too often?

15. Which alcohol do you think tastes the worst?

16. Do you know anyone who is a reformed alcoholic?

17. What do you think of groups like Alcoholics Anonymous? What are some other ways to help overcome a drinking problem?

18. Do you know anyone who has quit drinking **cold turkey**?

19. Do you know any symptoms attributed to alcohol **withdrawal**?

20. **What's your poison?** What alcoholic beverage do you usually drink?

21. Can you list some popular kinds of **hard liquor**?

22. What is the funniest thing you've ever seen someone do while **under the influence**?

23. What are some illnesses caused by **heavy drinking**?

24. What are some of the effects of heavy drinking on society?

25. Does alcohol make you more or less talkative?

26. Do you know any **happy drunks**?

27. Have you ever gotten into a **brawl** when you were drinking?

28. Do you have more fun when you drink?

29. Who is the heaviest drinker you know? How often do they drink?

30. Do you know anyone who has had **alcohol poisoning**? What happened to them?

31. Which country produces the best beer?

32. Have you ever gone on an all-night drinking **binge**? When was the last time?

For Abstainers

1. Why don't you drink?

2. Have you ever had a drink? How long have you been **sober**?

3. Do you think your country has a problem with over-consumption of alcohol. If so, how can this problem be fixed?

4. Is drinking engrained in your country's culture? Is it possible to change this?

5. Do you **frown on** people who enjoy drinking?

6. How would you handle a boss who insisted you drink with him/her?

7. Do you know any other **teetotalers**?

8. Are people who **abstain** generally healthier than people who drink?

9. Are social drinkers generally healthy?

10. Are there any occasions, such as holidays, on which it is okay to have a social drink?

11. Some people don't drink because of their religion; however, other members of the same religion do drink? Why?

12. In your opinion what constitutes a heavy drinker? How much and how often do they drink?

13. What are some illnesses caused by heavy drinking?

14. What are some of the effects of heavy drinking on society?

15. Can you think of some economic effects of heavy drinking?

16. Do people who drink have more fun? Why or why not?

17. Do you think the legal age for drinking should be raised? Why or why not?

18. What do you think of groups like Alcoholics Anonymous?

19. What do you think of the idea of **prohibition**?

20. How will you convince your children not to drink?

21. Is it okay to have an occasional glass of wine?

22. Do any of your relatives drink? Are any of them heavy drinkers?

23. Are you embarrassed when you see a friend who is drunk?

24. Generally, how do you feel when you see someone passed out on the street?

25. Are you disgusted when you see people being sick on the street?

26. How do you feel when you see young people carrying each other onto the subway?

27. Who is the most obnoxious drunk you have ever met?

28. What do you usually drink when you go out with your friends?

16 Socializing and Making Friends

Language Points

an acquaintance / friend / close friend / old friend / pal / buddy / mate / chum
> I have many acquaintances, but only a few close friends

to meet someone somewhere / to meet someone for something
> I met my best friend at university. I'm meeting him tonight for dinner.

to get to know someone (well)
> Whenever I meet new people, it takes me a long time to get to know them.

to get along (well) with someone
> What kind of people do you get along best with?

to go out for drinks / dinner with someone
> There aren't many people I go out for drinks with on a regular basis.

to hang out with someone
> I don't usually hang out with people from work.

to keep in touch with someone
> I haven't kept in touch with my friends from elementary school.

to get together with someone (for something)
> Every Friday, I get together with my college buddies for drinks.

to take someone out (to) somewhere for something
> It's his birthday, so we're all taking him out to MacDougall's for drinks.

to invite someone over / out / out for something / to do something
> Why don't we invite Bill over for dinner tonight?

to get in touch (with someone) / to be in touch (with someone) / to get back in touch (with someone)
> I'm glad that you and Jeremy are back in touch. You were such good friends for such a long time.

Dialogue

A husband is bringing in the groceries.

Sam: You'll never guess who I **bumped into** at Loblaw's today!

Grace: Who?

Sam: Jerry. You remember Jerry...my old fishing **buddy**?

Grace: Oh, we **haven't seen him in ages**!

Sam: Yeah. But you know, he **hasn't aged a day**. He still looks exactly the same. He's still driving that same **beat up** old Volkswagen. **Same old Jerry**.

Grace: So, how is he? Is he still married to that...what was her name? Isn't that crazy? We used to be **bosom pals** and now I can't even remember her name!

Sam: You mean Deborah?

Grace: Right, Deborah. It was **on the tip of my tongue**. Are they still together?

Sam: Nope. Divorced. He has really **let himself go**, too. He **looked like hell**.

Grace: Aw, that's a shame. They made a nice couple. Well, he must **have a lot of time on his hands** now. We should invite him for dinner.

Sam: No way! Are you crazy?

Grace: Well, I just thought...

Sam: Don't you remember the last time we invited Jerry over? He **drank like a fish, hit on** every woman in the room, and **made a complete ass of himself**. I was **mortified**.

Grace: Oh, that's right. Your parents were there, too. Well, why don't we **let bygones be bygones** and invite him for dinner on Friday?

Sam: Hmm...alright, but **don't say I didn't warn you**.

Comprehension

1. Briefly explain in your own words what Sam and Grace are talking about.

2. What is Sam's opinion of Jerry?

3. What does Grace mean by 'let bygones be bygones'?

4. Do you have any friends that your family or spouse do not approve of? How do you keep the peace?

5. Are there any friends you've lost touch with? Why do you think you haven't been able to keep in touch?

6. Do you think that it is easy or difficult for married people to be friends with single or divorced people? Why?

Throughout our lives, our idea of what makes someone a good friend might change, but the general principles remain the same.

In kindergarten, good friends might have let us have the red crayon, instead of the **yucky** black one. They were the ones who seemed able to play with us for extended periods without it turning into **all out war**. They were the ones who shared their precious snacks with us at lunchtime.

In childhood, good friends were the people who were always there to sit with us at lunchtime, or the people who always wanted to walk home with us after school. They were the people who laughed at our **antics**, when everyone else thought we were just being idiotic.

In **adolescence**, good friends let us copy their homework, risked punishment to pass us notes in class, always managed to get the seat next to us, and never revealed who we secretly had a crush on.

As a teenager, our good friends were probably our partners in **naughtiness**. They helped us laugh through the rough world of growing up, stood by and cheered on our successes, and picked us up and dusted us off after the sting of disappointment or **betrayal**.

As adults, good friends are those who are dependable, always ready with a listening ear, and words of encouragement, or advice. Good friends remember our birthdays. Good friends are the people we want to call when something has got us down, or when things suddenly seem to be falling apart. Good friends don't let us take ourselves too seriously. They let us be ourselves, but also help us grow to become better people.

Common Ground

When we meet someone for the first time, conversation usually revolves around areas of common interest. Work with your classmate(s). Focus your discussion on the areas listed below and try to find things that you have in common with them. Take notes, and be prepared to let the rest of the class know what sort of common ground you've discovered. For example, you might want to make statements like the following.

Both Janice and Marissa liked the Matrix.
Neither Jenna nor I particularly like reading magazines.

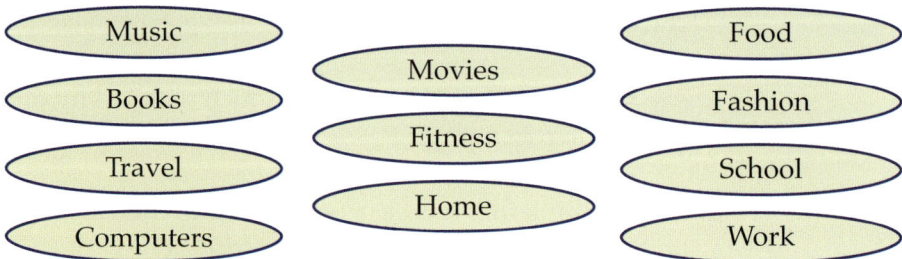

The Social Anxiety Quiz

Are you good at socializing? With your classmate(s), answer the questions in this quiz and then discuss the results.

		Yes	No
❶	Do you feel tense around people you don't know?		
❷	When in a group, do you try to be the centre of attention?		
❸	Do you think you are successful socially?		
❹	Do you find performing in public (singing, telling a joke, dancing) difficult?		
❺	Do you find it difficult to speak in front of groups?		
❻	Are you satisfied with the image you present to others?		
❼	Would you eat alone in a crowded restaurant?		
❽	Do you think you are good at socializing?		
❾	When someone gives you praise, are you able to receive it comfortably and naturally?		
❿	When you meet strangers, do you listen more than speak?		
⓫	Do you express your feelings to friends, even if your relationship isn't very close yet?		
⓬	Do you turn red when someone shouts to get your attention in public?		
⓭	Do you feel a sense of inferiority when you're introduced to an important person?		
⓮	Do you often think that your contributions to a debate can be relevant?		
⓯	When you are going to be introduced to a group of unfamiliar people, do you sweat, shake a bit, and feel insecure?		
⓰	Would you be able to imitate a famous person in front of a group?		

Calculate your score.

- If you said YES to questions 1, 5, 10, 12, 13 and 15, give yourself a point for each YES.
- If you said NO to questions 2, 3, 4, 6, 7, 8, 9, 11, 14 and 16, give yourself a point for each NO.

If you scored less than 6, your ability to make friends is acceptable.
Between 6 and 10: you have/have had difficulty relating to other people socially.
More than 10 points: new situations and getting to know new people is hard for you.

1. Describe one of your closest friends.

2. Do you have any childhood friendships that are still strong today? Tell us about them. Which friend have you known the longest? How did the two of you meet? How often do you see each other these days? Have you ever had any major disagreements with him/her? What do you have in common?

3. Are there any long lost friends you'd like to **get back in touch with**? What stops you from getting back in touch with them?

4. Have you ever fallen out with any of your friends? What happened? Have you made up?

5. Do you have any long distance friends?

6. What friendships are more durable: friendships between guys, or friendships between girls?

7. Do you make friends easily?

8. How many people do you consider your "best friends?"

9. What makes a friendship last a long time?

10. Is it common to have friendships across generations? Do you have any good friends who are significantly older or younger than you?

11. Do you think that friends should have a lot in common? Is it important that your friends come from the same country, share the same opinions with you, and come from the same social class?

12. Do you usually **hang out with** the same group of close friends or with many different people?

13. Describe a perfect evening with friends. Where would you go? What would you do? How much time (and money) would you spend? What time would the evening begin and end?

14. Where is a good place to meet new friends?

15. Who is the most interesting person you have ever met?

16. Do you think men and women can be friends? How about after marriage? Should married people have friends of the opposite sex?

17. Where is a good place to meet a new boyfriend/girlfriend?

18. If you lived in a foreign country, would the way you socialize be different? Are there any differences between the way people in your country and people from foreign countries spend time together?

19. Do you have any friends of a different nationality? Are there any advantages of having a friend of a different nationality?

20. Do you usually socialize with people from work? From school? From your temple or church?

21. In your country, is it common to invite groups of people to one's house for a dinner party, a potluck party, pool party, or barbeque? If not, why are these sorts of social gatherings uncommon?

22. How does alcohol influence the way people socialize?

23. What kinds of people do you **get along well with**? Are there any sorts of people you don't normally **get along with**?

24. If you had a serious problem, who would you be most likely to talk to about it first: a family member or a close friend?

25. Do you think it is possible to overcome shyness? How?

26. What makes someone a great conversationalist?

27. Do you enjoy gossiping? Who do you usually gossip about? Have you gossiped today? Yesterday? What did you gossip about?

17 Money

Language Points

to make / earn (an amount of) money
> She earns 60 grand a year.

to save (up)(an amount of) money (for something)
> They haven't saved enough money for that summerhouse they want.

to spend (some amount of) money (on something)
> Did you really spend that much (money) on his birthday present?

to budget one's money
> They finally took a course to learn how to budget their money.

to lend money to someone / to lend someone money
> Don't lend him any money!

to borrow money from someone
> He's always borrowing money from his friends.

to pay someone back (an amount of) money
> And he never pays anyone back.

to repay (someone) (an amount of) money
> I've asked him to repay me several times.

to be in debt
> He always says that he is deeply in debt.

Dialogue

Two friends are talking about a mutual acquaintance.

Jane: Oh, you know who I bumped into at the movie theatre? Ellen..

Sunny: Oh, really? She's been avoiding me for weeks. What did she have to say?

Jane: She said she's been really busy lately. She talked about how she never has time to see her friends anymore. And she told me to tell you that she's really sorry about not calling you.

Sunny: Huh? Really? Is that what she said? I guess **she didn't mention how much money she owes me**.

Jane: No, she didn't. Is that true?

Sunny: Sure. **She asked me if I'd lend her two thousand dollars for the down payment on a car she was buying.** She...

Jane: She asked you for <u>how</u> much?!

Sunny: Two thousand. Why? What's the matter?

Jane: And you <u>gave</u> it to her?! You know how bad Ellen is with money. That was a bad move on your part. You know, the other day, she told me that she'd gone out shopping and bought herself a whole bunch of new outfits.

Sunny: Well, at the time, **she told me not to worry and that she'd pay me back in a week when she got her paycheck**. That was two months ago, and I haven't heard a thing from her. She never answers her phone, and she won't return my messages or e-mails. She's obviously avoiding me.

Jane: What are you going to do?

Sunny: What <u>can</u> I do?

Jane: Not much, I guess. Well, hopefully you've learned your lesson. **A good friend of mine once suggested that I should never lend money to anyone.** I always follow that advice and I've never run into any trouble.

Sunny: Hey, I told you that!

Comprehension

1. What were Jane and Sunny talking about?

2. What did their friend Ellen do?

3. What would you do if you were in this situation?

Activity A

Money Idioms

These days, everyone is chasing the **almighty** dollar. Fortunes are made and lost **in the blink of an eye**, and **split-second decisions** often make the difference between success and failure. Money has been a **key** element in our society for thousands of years, and it will continue to play a **vital** role in the future.

Have a look at these proverbs related to money. Using examples, explain what each one means.

- A fool and his money are soon parted.
- Money doesn't grow on trees.
- Everyone has their price.
- Money talks.
- Money is the root of all evil.

- Lend your money and lose your friend.
- You can't take it with you when you go.   ● Time is money.
- The more you get, the more you want.
- Penny wise and pound foolish.
- If you look after the pennies, the dollars will look after themselves.

Part1. Reading : Stranded in Las Vegas

A desparate son has written the following email to his parents. Read the email, then discuss the meanings of the expressions in boldface with the class.

File Edit View Go Message Tools Window Help

Get Msgs Compose Reply Reply All Forward Next Junk Delete

Subject: [SMTPAppender] Application message
From: log4j@server5
Date: 4:09 PM
To: neo@localhost

Dear Mom and Dad,

Hi. I am having a good time here in Las Vegas. The weather has been great, and I have met a lot of people. My classes are going pretty well so far I guess. I should receive some of my marks next week. Unfortunately, I am **running a little short** of money. I **ran up a** huge phone **bill** last month, so I have no choice but to send you an e-mail. I was **getting by** all right on the **allowance** that you sent me, and I even **earned** a little extra **pocket money** working at the library on the weekends. However, I don't **get paid** until the 20th, so I am wondering if you guys can **lend** me some cash to **tide me over** until then?

I must confess that I've **blown a lot of money** at the casino since I arrived here. My credit cards are **maxed-out**, I've already **dipped into my savings** account, and I am **flat broke** now. I **borrowed** some money from my friend, Jeff, and I still haven't **paid him back**. He told me to **cough up** the money by next Wednesday, or else... I'm really **hard up** for cash! I know what you are going to say - that I need to **budget** my money and start **cutting a few corners**. I promise you though that if you **bail me out** just this once, I will never ask you for money again!

Love,
Sang Woo

Part2. Put Your Money Where Your Mouth Is

		Expression
❶	Do you often **spend a lot of money wastefully** on non-essential items?	
❷	When you were a child, how much **extra money for enjoyment** did you get per week?	
❸	Is it embarrassing to ask a friend for money to **help you live until you get some more money**?	
❹	Have you ever been in a position where you found it difficult to **manage financially**?	
❺	What is the largest amount you've ever **accumulated** on your phone bill?	
❻	Do you think that you could **survive on a limited amount of money**?	
❼	Are you often tempted **to start spending money** you have put aside?	
❽	If you were completely **without money**, what would be the hardest things to do without?	
❾	Can you think of situations where **economizing on non-essential items** can be risky?	
❿	If a friend with gambling debts asked you to **help him out of his difficult financial situation**, what would you do?	

Credit Card Debate

You will be asked to defend one of the following positions. Before you begin, read over the supporting arguments, and choose what you will focus your argument on. Remember to listen carefully to opposing positions and respond to their points. Wherever possible, give examples and facts to back up your argument.

Opinion 1: Credit Cards Are Essential

- There are now a number of everyday activities, such as buying things on-line, which are not possible without a credit card.

- Customers can stop payment on a credit card account for unsatisfactory services.

- Most credit card companies offer purchase points and merchandise incentives, or airfare mileage points.

- Credit cards are a perfect way to establish and maintain a good credit rating.

- Using credit cards, you can re-establish your credit rating after bankruptcy or other financial mishaps.

- Credit cards allow you to get cash advances for emergencies.

Opinion 2: The Risks of Having Credit Cards Outweigh the Benefits

- The temptation to acquire too many credit card accounts can lead to losing track of payment details and deadlines.

- Credit cards give people a false sense of security and freedom, which makes them likely to overspend.

- Most people who have credit cards have difficulty understanding the details about how the various fees are calculated.

- Young people, especially, are often poor at managing their money, and likely to find themselves in personal bankruptcy.

- Credit card companies often charge high interest rates on cash advances.

Roommates on a Shoestring

You and your classmate(s) are sharing an apartment and have pooled your money to pay for your necessities. Your rent, utilities, and basic groceries have already been paid for, and you've only got $200 left. You're going to have to think about how to make it last until your next payday. From the list below, select the things that you feel you simply cannot do without, and consider how many you will need to get you through the month. If you want to spend money on non-essential (N) items, you'll need to justify the purchase with your classmate(s). Negotiate with your partner(s) to make your budget work.

	Item	Price per unit ($)	Quantity	Cost ($)
N	Dry-cleaning / ironing	$4		
	Soap and shampoo	$6		
N	Underarm deodorant	$3		
	Toothpaste	$3		
	Toilet paper (12 rolls)	$6		
	Kitchen / bathroom cleaner	$4		
	Dishwashing liquid / scouring pad	$5		
N	Movie tickets (a pair)	$12		
N	DVD rental	$1		
N	Taxi fare	$3		
	Bus / Subway fare	$1		
N	Snack food	$1		
N	Take-out meal	$10		
N	Restaurant meal	$20		
N	A bottle of wine	$10		
N	A case of beer (6 cans)	$8		
N	Soft drink (2 litre bottle)	$2		
N	Cigarettes (1 pack)	$2		
N	A haircut	$15		
N	A Trip to the sauna	$2		
N	A trip to the Internet café	$4		

Total:

1. Have you ever been **hard up** for money? What did you do to **scrape by**?

2. Have you ever lent money to a friend who was **broke**? If a friend didn't pay you back for a long time, how would you handle the situation?

3. If you suddenly became **filthy rich**, what would you buy first? How do you think your lifestyle would change? Would you still work? Do you think there would be bad as well as good consequences?

4. Why are people so concerned with being **well off**? Does money always bring happiness? Explain your opinion.

5. What is the most you have ever **blown** on a **shopping spree**? How about for a meal? On alcohol? On a gift for someone special?

6. Do you and your friends usually **chip in** to pay the tab when you go out, or does someone usually **foot the bill** themselves? Have you ever **gotten stuck with the bill** unexpectedly?

7. How much time do you spend **budgeting** your money? Do you use home budgeting software, an accounting book, or some other method? What are your reasons for budgeting/not budgeting your money?

8. Have you ever been **ripped off**? What were you buying?

9. Are you a **bargain hunter**? Are you good at **haggling**? Give an example of a time that you negotiated a very good deal.

10. Are you an **impulse buyer**? Do you sometimes buy things you don't need or can't afford? If so, give examples.

11. Are you **saving up** for anything special these days? How much money do you **put aside** each month?

12. How much cash do you usually **carry on you**? How about when you travel?

13. How often do you pay for things by credit card? How many credit cards do you have? Are any of them **maxed out**? Or are you good at managing your credit card spending? If so, what's your secret?

14. When you buy something expensive, do you pay for it in **installments**, or do you usually pay for it all at once.

15. How many bank accounts do you have? What do you use each of them for?

16. Do you think couples should have **joint bank accounts**? Many people also have a secret account that they don't tell their spouse about. Do you think this is a good idea?

17. Do you invest in the stock market? Do you think it is risky?

18. If you were forced to **cut corners**, what would you be willing to give up? (Ex. your cell phone, driving, dining out, drinking, going to the movies, etc.)

19. In your opinion, what's the best way to make a lot of money?

20. At what age do you think people should be expected to be financially independent from their families? What do you think of young people who live at home after they start working and continue to **sponge off** their parents?

18 The Future

Language Points

on the horizon
> I think that there are some good things on the horizon for me. I'm beginning a new job next month, and I'm planning to get married next year.

in the near future
> I'm beginning a new career at a great company in the near future. I'm really excited about it.

in the not too distant future
> Life expectancy is increasing very quickly, so I think that in the not-too-distant future, many people, especially many women, will be living to the age of 100.

in the short run / in the long run
> In the short run, I will be studying hard to improve my test scores and develop my English skills. In the long run, I hope to have a successful career at a great company.

short-term / medium-term / long-term
> My short-term goal is to get great test scores. My medium-term goal is to get a good job at a great company. My long-term goal is to own my own company and become rich.

it's still in the early days
> Things are working out really well with my new girlfriend, but it's still in the early days. It's too soon to say whether or not we'll be getting married.

for good
> Some people might be willing to move abroad to find a good job, but I love it here and I plan on staying here for good.

long way off
> Some day we might be able to eat strawberries that are the size of apples, but that day is still a long way off.

Reading

Predictions for the Year 2000

In the year 1900, a journalist named John Watkins, Jr. asked the most famous American scientists and professors for their predictions on changes that would occur during the next century. Read the predictions that were made for the year 2000, and answer the following questions:

1. Which predictions have come true?

2. Which might come true **in the near future**?

3. Are we still **in the early days of** some of the predictions?

4. Which predictions are **still a long way off**?

5. Which predictions can never be accomplished?

6. Which predictions would you like to come true?

Human Development and Health

- Americans will be 1 to 2 inches (2.5-5 centimeters) taller, and live to age 50.
- Doctors will be able to view the inside of the human body. Invisible light rays will let doctors see a heart inside the chest, and to magnify and photograph any part of it.

Transportation

- Automobiles will have replaced every horse vehicle. There will be automobile police patrols, automobile ambulances, and automobile street sweepers.
- There will be no automobiles on the streets of large cities. All traffic will be below ground (in subways or tunnels) or high above ground.
- Trains will run 2 miles (3.2 kilometers) a minute; express trains 150 miles an hour (240 kilometers an hour).
- There will be air-ships, mainly to make war and to transport people and goods. Scientists will use the airships to make observations from high above the earth.
- Electric ships, crossing the ocean at more than a mile (1.6 kilometers) a minute, will travel from America to England in two days.
- Flying refrigerators will bring fresh summer fruits from the tropics in the winter.

Technology

- Photographs will be telegraphed all across the world. Photos from distant battles will be published in the newspapers an hour later. Photos will show all of nature's colors.
- We will see live, moving pictures from around the world. Cameras, often thousands of miles apart, will transmit the pictures. A giant telephone will transmit live sound.
- Wireless telephone circuits will extend around the world.
- The temperature of a house will be regulated by turning on hot or cold air from a faucet.
- Scientists will have discovered how to grow fruits currently grown only in much hotter or colder climates.

Nature

- Mosquitoes, house-flies and roaches will have been exterminated. Governments will have destroyed (often with the use of chemicals) or drained all mosquito breeding-grounds, such as stagnant pools, swamp-lands, and still-water streams.
- There will be no wild animals except in zoos. Rats and mice will have been exterminated.
- Strawberries and raspberries will grow as big as apples.
- There will be black, blue and green roses. It will be possible to grow any flower in any color and to transfer the perfume of scented flowers to odorless ones.

Education and the English Language

- There will be no C, X or Q in the English alphabet because they are unnecessary. Spelling based on the sound of words will have been adopted.
- English will be the most widely spoken language. Russian will be second.
- A university education will be free to all men and women.

Activity A

Think of the changes that the world will be experiencing between now and the end of the century. Write predictions on each of the topics below.

people's health	education and school
transportation	work and job market trends
science and technology	medicine and medical technology
nature, the environment, and environmental problems	family and relationships

Examples

By the year 2100...

- *People will be living to age 100.*
- *We will be able to travel from New York to London in under 3 hours.*
- *Robots will perform most housework for us.*
- *The polar ice caps will have melted, and coastal cities will have been flooded.*
- *The summer and winter vacations will have been eliminated. Students will go to school year-round.*
- *We will have a working day of four hours.*
- *Scientists will have found a cure for most forms of cancer.*
- *Low birthrates will have caused the population of most countries to shrink.*

Read your predictions to your partner(s), and discuss each other's predictions. Then with your partner, decide which of your predictions are the most likely to come true. Be prepared to tell the class which predictions you and your partner have decided are the most likely to occur.

The World in 2050

Read the following predictions for the year 2050. Write "A" beside the sentences that you agree with, and "D" beside the sentences that you disagree with. Then work in pairs or small groups, and share your opinions on whether you agree or disagree with the predictions.

Career and Work Life Trends

a The "company man" will become rare or disappear completely. Few people will be employed "for life" by a single company. Even highly-educated people will have to change jobs frequently.

b There will be many good, high-paying jobs.

c There will be fewer jobs, and more competition to get and keep a job. Highly skilled professionals will have to work longer and longer hours to earn a good salary. Unskilled work will be done by machines, causing high unemployment among unskilled workers. Most jobs will either be high paying or low paying. The middle class will disappear.

d Men's dominance in certain career fields will disappear. Half of employees in medicine, science, technology and engineering will be women. Female CEOs and self-made female millionaires will be common. In politics, female presidents will be common.

e We'll be working less and will have more free time to enjoy our lives.

Educational Trends

a Many traditional schools will disappear and be replaced by online learning. Few university students will attend lectures. Instead, they will watch lectures at their convenience over the Internet.

b English mania has peaked. In the future most people will have to learn Chinese and Spanish to get a job.

c Government efforts to promote English in the classroom will be successful. Prior to entering university, students will study a range of subjects in English.

d When applying for a job, the importance of the name of your university will decline. Hiring companies will be more interested in your skills and talents, and less interested in the name of your university.

e The university entrance exam will become less important in determining which students are admitted to university. Other factors, such as high school GPA, will become more important.

Family and Relationships

a The main breadwinner in many families will be the woman.

b With many women having great jobs and high salaries, many women will decide not to get married. People will be marrying later in life or not at all.

c There will be a lot of intermarriage and many multicultural families, due to growing immigration, the spread of English fluency, more foreign travel, and changing attitudes.

d Fathers will become more involved in family life and raising children.

Health and Medical Technology

a Research breakthroughs will lead to cures for cancer, Alzheimer's and other deadly diseases. Many people will live to age 100.

b "Designer children" will be common. Genetic profiling will let parents select the sex and physical appearance of children.

c Technology and gadgets will encourage a sedentary lifestyle, so people will become much heavier. The average man will weigh at least 20 kilograms more, and the average woman at least 10 kilograms more.

d Many old people will have functioning artificial eyes and mechanical hearts.

Activity C

Talking about Your Classmates' Futures

Work in small groups. Find someone for whom each of the statements below is true. Be sure to ask further/follow-up questions. Be ready to tell the class about some of the most interesting answers that you have heard.

1. I will have taken some important exams by the end of this year.

2. I will have lost weight by the end of the year.

3. I will probably have enrolled at a school abroad by this time next year.

4. I will have started to study a new language by this time next year.

5. I will have found/started a new job by this time next year.

6. I will have taken a nice vacation by this time next year.

7. I will probably have gotten married by this time next year.

8. I will have left my home country **for good** to settle down in a foreign country by age 30.

9. I will have become a father/mother by age 35.

10. I will have created my own business by age 40.

Creating a Time Capsule

To help future generations understand life in your country in the early 21ˢᵗ century, you and your partner(s) are going to create a "time capsule" - a container that holds historical objects and historical records that represent current culture and society. The time capsule will not be opened until the year 2200.

A. Work alone and create a list of 15 items to be included in the time capsule.

Time Capsule Guidelines

- Include 15 items that represent typical life in your country in the early 21st century.

- The time capsule will be the size of a large suitcase.

- The time capsule will be sealed very effectively. It will be airtight. Even fresh food will be effectively preserved.

- Consider the main ideas you want to communicate. You might consider including items from the following categories:

¡ Culture and entertainment	¡ Technological gadgets
¡ Food and drink	¡ Media products (newspapers, magazines)
¡ Fashion and design	
¡ Current events and politics	¡ Objects that are important in everyday living
¡ Sports and games	

B. In pairs or small groups, discuss the items you have chosen. Choose the five best items for the time capsule.

C. Take turns with your partner(s) and explain to the class why you have chosen the five items on your list. You or your partner should write your list on the white board.

D. After all pairs and groups have presented their lists to the class, the whole class will vote on the ten best objects overall. Each student may vote for five objects.

Discussion

1. In your opinion, what problems are **on the horizon** for the society and the economy of your home country?

2. What are some things that do not currently exist that you would like to see invented **in the near future**?

3. What are your **short-term** and **long-term** professional and personal goals? Do you have a dream for the future? Do you think you can achieve your dream?

4. What are your career goals for **the long run**? What job do you expect to have in the year 2020?

5. In the year 2020, what kind of family do you expect to have? Where do you expect to live? Describe your life.

6. What will you be doing next winter vacation? Next summer vacation? Do you have any trips planned for the **not too distant future**?

7. Would you like to be transported into the future? How far? Why?

8. In the future, will people be living longer? If yes, how much longer?

9. Would you like to live to be 100 years old? Why or why not?

10. Do you think that you will look good for your age in the future?

11. Can fortune-tellers predict the future? Why do you think so? Why don't you think so?

12. Have you ever had a dream that foretold the future? What did you dream about?

13. How have your dreams for your future changed in recent years? Have your expectations for yourself increased or decreased?

14. What do you expect to be doing at this time next year?

15. Do you expect to see a major war in your lifetime? What do you think might be the causes?

16. Do you expect there to be more or less unemployment 10 years from now? Will the job market be better? What new industries will appear and develop?

17. Will the gap between rich and poor increase or decrease in the next ten years? State your opinion and reasons to support your opinion.

18. In your lifetime, will we find cures for cancer and other life-threatening diseases? What other health problems will arise?

19. What New Year's resolutions did you make last New Year? Have you been keeping them?

20. In what foreign countries do you expect to live in the future? Why?

21. If a time machine existed and you could go forward in time to any point in history, when and where would you go?

22. Complete the sentences

> This time next year, I'll be...
>
> By this time next year, I'll have...
>
> In five years' time, I'll be...
>
> By the time I am 50 years old, I'll have...

19 A Matter of Taste

to dine out / to eat out

My wife and I dine out about once a week.

connoisseur

I've become quite a connoisseur of steak. I know all the best restaurants.

a picky eater

I'm a bit of a picky eater, so my wife usually doesn't like to cook for me.

junk food

Since I went on my diet, I've been trying to avoid eating junk food.

fast food

Fast food is out of the question. It's far too fatty.

to pig out

Last night, I really pigged out at the restaurant, but it was all healthy food.

to wolf down / scoff down / devour

I was so hungry that I wolfed down a salad, a steak dinner, and a big slice of apple pie.

leftovers

I couldn't finish all the food we'd ordered, so there were lots of leftovers.

doggy bag / to "box" it / may I have it "to go"

The waiter was nice enough to give us a doggy bag, though.

Dialogue

Emily Richards, a professional restaurant reviewer, is being interviewed for a radio program.

Interviewer: Thank you for taking the time to talk with us today.

Emily: Oh, no problem. It's my pleasure.

Interviewer: I think that a lot of our listeners would love to have your job. How did you get into this field?

Emily: Well, food's been my primary interest **since day one**. I've been reviewing restaurants mentally for as long as I can remember. I ate out a lot as a kid, and I also worked in the restaurant industry for many years, so I've always had strong opinions about **what makes a restaurant tick**.

Interviewer: What sort of skills do you think a restaurant reviewer needs to possess?

Emily:	Well, a good skill to have would be a memory for flavours. I can recall meals I've eaten, even years afterward. Ask me what I ate on my vacation three years ago, and I could tell you every **appetizer, entrée**, and **garnish**. I can remember every bite. And, of course, you need to be able to write about it **descriptively**.
Interviewer:	Has anyone ever had a problem with a review you've written?
Emily:	Sure. I've gotten a couple of letters from restaurant owners. The letters are usually from insecure people who have trouble accepting criticism - people who think that no matter what, their place should be awarded four stars. I think I'd be a bit afraid if I was writing very harsh criticisms. That sort of thing **is bound to provoke** strong reactions. So when I'm very critical, I make sure my facts are **rock solid**. I'm always conscious that there are people out there **taking every word to heart**.
Interviewer:	When you're eating at a restaurant that you're reviewing, how do you mix work with pleasure?
Emily:	There's no pleasure. It's all work. While everyone else is enjoying **a night out**, I'm trying to look **inconspicuous** while I'm busy taking notes under the table.
Interviewer:	Is this still your dream job, or are there things you dislike about it?
Emily:	Hmm. Some nights I just **don't feel up to** eating at a restaurant. When **dining out** was something I did only occasionally, I used to get excited about it. But when it's three or four nights a week, it gets a little tiring. Sometimes, though, when I go to a new place, and I'm pleasantly surprised, I get excited about writing the column. It's a great job.
Interviewer:	Emily Richards, thank you.

Comprehension

1. What qualities or qualifications does Emily Richards think a food critic should possess?

2. From what she says, do you get the impression that she likes her job? Why or why not?

3. Do you think that you would enjoy doing her job? Why or why not?

4. Do you ever read restaurant reviews?

5. Would you be likely to try a new restaurant if you read a favourable review of it? Would you stay away from a restaurant that received an unfavourable review?

6. What are some of the things that you expect from a restaurant?

7. What is your favourite restaurant and why do you like it?

8. Have you ever had a terrible dining experience? What made it terrible?

No matter how it's prepared, how much or how little of it we eat, whether we are picky eaters or willing to try anything, food is a very important part of everyone's life. Biologically and psychologically, food is of the highest importance to our health and well-being.

But beyond this, the kinds of food we eat also serve to identify us as members of a particular culture. What foreigners might find **distasteful** or even **revolting**, the locals of an area consider normal. For example, you might find it disgusting that people would eat insects, but in some parts of the world, people eat insects without giving it a second thought.

Sometimes these cultural differences are not only a matter of taste but become the subject of debates about morality. Some people find it objectionable that some Europeans eat horse or rabbit or that some Asian cultures eat monkey, cat, or dog.

In this age of globalization, some people are becoming increasingly concerned that the spread of Western fast food culture is threatening to **obscure** their native food culture. In countries all over the world, young people, especially, are becoming **accustomed** to eating American-style food instead of their native **cuisine**.

Activity A

Dinner Party

Some important people are arriving in a few days from out of town and your class would like to impress them. Work with your classmate(s) to plan a dinner party to welcome them on their first night in your country. Use the following chart to help you plan. Next, make a presentation to the class and try to convince them that the meal you have planned would be the most suitable.

Location	_____	
Who Will Cook?	☐ A professional cook	☐ Myself
	☐ My mother/ grandmother	☐ Other _____
Type of Cuisine	☐ Korean	☐ Italian
	☐ Japanese	☐ French
	☐ Chinese	☐ Turkish
	☐ American	☐ Other _____
Style of Food	☐ Haute Cuisine	☐ Home-cooking
	☐ Rustic/Traditional	☐ Other _____
Number of Courses	_____	

Menu	☐ Hors D'oeuvres _____
	☐ Soup _____
	☐ Salad _____
	☐ Entree _____
	☐ Side Dish(es) _____
	☐ Dessert _____
	☐ Other _____
	☐ Other _____
Beverages	☐ Aperitif _____
	☐ Accompaniment _____
	☐ Digestif _____
Estimated Cost (per person)	_____
Other Features	_____
	_____
	_____
	_____

Activity B

Eat Your Words

Work with your classmate(s). Describe, in as much detail as possible, each of the following. Focus on describing smells, tastes, and other sensations, as well as ingredients and methods of preparation.

Your favorite beverage

The strangest thing you've ever eaten

A food you could never give up

The best meal you've ever had at a restaurant

A food you were forced to eat as a child

What you typically eat for breakfast

Your mother's speciality

Something you can cook well

A cooking experiment that went horribly wrong

Consumption Trends

Discuss the following trends with your classmate(s). For each one, speculate about what has caused these trends, what the consequences are, whether they should be reversed, and how this could be done.

Many children prefer Western fast food to traditional food.

Children and teenagers are getting fatter these days.

Anorexia and other eating disorders are becoming more common, especially among young women.

Women are smoking and drinking more than they used to.

Increasingly, young people, including high school and university students, are taking up smoking.

How Hungry Are You?

You and your partner(s) have been stranded in a remote and mountainous region after a plane crash. According to your best estimates, it should take about a week for help to reach you. You've managed to scrounge together some edible items to keep you going until help arrives. Each has an energy value (how long it will satisfy your hunger). From the list, pick the items (in order of preference) that you would be willing to eat. Then try to trade the remaining items from your 'food supply' with your classmate(s) until everyone has at least 100 hours of food energy. Also think about how the food could be made more appetizing.

		Edible Items per Person		
Quantity	Item	Unit	Total energy value (hours)	Order of Preference
3	Passengers' half-eaten cabin meals (rotten)	1 meal	6	
125	Non-dairy coffee creamers	25 creamers	3	
3	Passengers' half-eaten packs of peanuts	1 pack	2	
Lots	Cockroaches	5 roaches	6	
Lots	Flies	15 flies	2	
Lots	Earthworms	8 worms	3	
Lots	Leaves and grass	2 cups	2	
10 cups	Unidentified berries (could be poisonous)	2 cups	2	
5	Mice	1 mouse	2	
Lots	Plant roots and bark	2 cups	6	
2	Rats	1 rat	2	
4	Pigeons	1 pigeon	4	
1	Yogurt cup (gone off)	1 cup	3	
4	Body parts of fellow passengers	1 limb	9	
1 tin (50 scoops)	Powdered hot chocolate	10 scoops	3	
2	Mini chocolate bars	1 bar	0.5	

Food for Thought

1. If you had to choose one food that is typical of your country, what would it be? Give reasons for your choice.

2. What kinds of food (Italian, Thai, Korean, French, etc.) do you enjoy eating? Are there any you would like to try?

3. Do you think that the food from your country is healthier than food from other countries? Why?

4. Do you think that you have healthy or unhealthy eating habits? Why?

5. How is your cooking? Do you cook? Do you cook well? What food do you cook most often? Is your mother / father a good cook?

6. Is drinking alcohol a part of the culture in your country? What are your favorite drinks? Is there anything that you hate?

7. Where do you usually eat when you go out for a meal? What are some of your favorite restaurants? What is your favorite bar or cafe / coffee shop? Why do you like it?

8. How often do you eat in fast food restaurants? What do you think about fast food?

9. Do you think that people's tastes in food are being Americanized? Are people losing an important part of their cultural identity?

10. Which food from your country do you like the least?

11. If you have lived abroad, what food from your country did you miss the most? If you were living abroad, what food would you miss the most?

12. Do you prefer to eat at a restaurant or at home?

13. What is your **comfort food**?

14. What do you think of vegetarianism and **veganism**?

15. What do you know about **GM food**? Do you approve of it?

Give Me a Break

to be stressed out / something stresses someone out

    These days, I'm really stressed out by my workload.

to deal with / cope with / manage / handle / reduce stress

    I work so much overtime that I don't have time to do things to cope with stress.

demanding

    And taking care of our new baby is also demanding.

anxiety

    I also feel a lot of anxiety about my future with this company.

a nervous wreck

    I'm a nervous wreck. I can't eat. I'm always jittery.

high blood pressure

    My blood pressure is sky-high.

irritable

    I'm so irritable these days. I snap at people for the smallest things.

fatigued

    I feel really fatigued all the time, as if I'm wearing a lead weight around my neck.

insomnia

    I also have bouts of insomnia, so that I can't sleep for days at a time.

stress level

    My wife is always telling me that I have to reduce my stress level, but how?

workaholic

    She says that I'm a workaholic, and I shouldn't accept so much responsibility.

burned out

    She's worried that I'm going to get burned out if I keep working like this.

Reading

There's no doubt about it: stress is one of the most common features of modern life. While it's true that people in the past were also stressed, stress has now become a distinctive characteristic of daily life. The reason why people these days suffer even more tension than their ancestors did is one of life's complexities When you think about it, the **sheer number** of choices facing people on a daily basis is **jarring**. From marriage and children to careers and hobbies, we have more choices facing us than we can sometimes handle. The result is stress. So, how stressed are you? Care to know? Have a look at the following simple stress test to get an idea.

Stress Test

Answer each question using a number. When you have completed the questionnaire, add up your total number of points. An answer key is provided on the next page. Discuss the results.

1 = Never True   2 = Sometimes True   3 = Often True   4 = Always True

1. I try to do as much as I can in the time I have.
2. I dislike being interrupted and sometimes become irritable.
3. If I don't win at games, I don't really have a good time playing them.
4. I speed to get through intersections before the light turns red.
5. I don't like to ask for help with a problem.
6. The respect and admiration of others is very important to me.
7. I often check the time.
8. I look for ways of doing better and achieving more.
9. I don't have enough time to do the things I need to do.
10. I do more than one thing at a time.
11. I get angry or irritable.
12. I don't spend time alone or have time to enjoy my hobbies.
13. I dislike talking with people who speak slowly.
14. I work at or near my limit.
15. My friends and relatives think I work at or near my limit.
16. I am involved in several projects at the same time.
17. I do most of my work to meet a deadline.
18. If I am not doing something, I feel uneasy or guilty.
19. I take on too many responsibilities.
20. I am dissatisfied with the way other people do their work.

TOTAL SCORE _____

Activity B

Could You Handle It?

Which of the following occupations do you think is the most stressful? Which do you think is the least stressful? Which ones could you handle? Rate each of the occupations below in order of most to least stressful. Discuss the demands of each job with your partner(s) and which aspects are the most and least stressful, and why you think so.

Occupation	Stress Ranking	Could You Handle It?	
		Yes	**No**
A high school teacher			
A taxi driver in a large city			
A high school student			
An accountant			
An air traffic controller			
A computer games developer			
A lion tamer			
An English Instructor			
An emergency room surgeon			
A politician			

Activity C

Pushing The Limits

Most people would find the following situations stressful in one way or another. With your classmate(s) discuss ways of approaching each situation that could reduce or alleviate the stress.

The couple that live across the hall from you are fighting like cat and dog. It's been going on for two hours and shows no signs of letting up.

You are asked at the last minute to give a presentation in front of a large group of people. You haven't had any time to prepare.

Your neighbours are having a noisy party, and it's 3:30 in the morning.

You accidentally bump the car ahead of you at a traffic light. There seems to be no damage, but the man gets out and starts yelling and swearing.

When you get to the airport to leave for your vacation, you find out that the flight has been delayed six hours.

Your apartment is broken into. They've taken everything of value.

You sit down to do your accounting at the end of the month, and realize that there is absolutely no way that you can cover all of your expenses.

You are driving to an important meeting that is scheduled to start in a few minutes. Suddenly you hit a traffic jam. You try to call to let them know you'll be late but find that your cell phone battery is dead.

The seat you've been assigned for your 16-hour flight is right next to a young mother with a crying baby and a hyperactive 4 year old.

Discussion

1. When you **are feeling stressed out**, what kinds of symptoms do you show? Do you withdraw from people? Sleep more? Sleep less? Suffer from **insomnia**? Feel **fatigued**? Become **irritable**? Smoke more? Eat more? Experience muscle tension or pain? Get headaches?

2. What causes you the most stress? Family, relationships, work, colleagues, romance, personal issues?

3. How do you **deal with stress**? Is it a healthy way to **deal with it**? Does your way of **dealing with** it lead to more stress?

4. What is the key to **reducing stress** in life? Exercise? Balance? Sleep?

5. Do you think that having some stress is a good thing? Why or why not?

6. Someone once said, "Having no stress is stressful." What does this mean? Do you agree?

7. Do you work long hours? Are you a **workaholic**? How does your long work week affect you personally?

8. Have you participated in any physical activity to reduce your stress? How about yoga, tai chi, or meditation?

9. What is your perspective on drinking to relieve stress?

10. Does smoking really **reduce stress**? Why do so many people use stress as an excuse to smoke?

11. Which would you choose and why: a fast-paced, exciting, but very stressful job in a large city, or a relaxed, fulfilling, sometimes boring job in the country?

12. Do you find that the lifestyle in your country is becoming more and more rushed and hectic? Are you satisfied with this lifestyle, or would you like to see things become more relaxed? If you suddenly became president or prime minister of your country, and could change something to make your country less stressful, what would you change? If you're happy with the lifestyle, explain why.

Appendix - Grammar and Usage

In this section, you can find resources related to some of the problems with grammar and usage you might encounter when discussing the topics in this book. Your teacher may refer to this material or you might want to study it on your own in preparation for class.

1 Usage: A Distinct Disadvantage

You can say that someone "has" an advantage or disadvantage "over" someone else.

- Korean children who grow up in Western countries <u>have an advantage over</u> those who don't.

You can also say that something "gives" someone or "puts" someone "at" an advantage or disadvantage.

- A lack of money and opportunities puts Korean children from lower income families <u>at a disadvantage</u>.

But you should <u>not</u> say that someone "gets" an advantage or disadvantage or that something "gets" someone an advantage or disadvantage.

- ✗ He got an advantage from having a Western father.
- He <u>gave</u> him an advantage.

Native speakers don't use the superlatives "best" or "most" when talking about advantages or disadvantages. They do, however, use the superlatives "biggest" or "greatest".

- ✗ My <u>best advantage</u> is my ability to speak English.
- My greatest advantage is my ability to speak English.

2 Usage: Keep In Touch

The words "in touch" figure prominently in many English idioms and are often used to mean "in contact with," as in the following examples:

- Did you get in touch with Shelly?
  (Did you contact Shelly?)

- When you go abroad make sure you keep in touch.
  (When you go abroad make sure you keep in contact with us.)

- I lost touch with him after high school.
  (We stopped contacting each other after high school.)

3 Grammar: I Don't Think That's Not Right

Have a look at the following sentences.

- I don't think he's not a nice guy. (= "I think he's a nice guy")
- Everybody doesn't like it. (= "Nobody likes it")
- Nobody doesn't like it. (= "Everybody likes it")

Sentences like these are called "double negatives" and are extremely confusing for both the listener and the speaker. You should avoid them altogether.

4 Grammar: How Can I Get This Right?

You should be careful when using the words "how" and "do". "How" asks about method and "do" is non-specific, which means it can be any action. Therefore the questions "How can/should I do?" and "How would you do in that situation?" are wrong. The problem is that if someone doesn't know what you want to do (remember "do" can be ANY action) they cannot tell you "how" you should do it. The correct questions would be:

- What can/should I do?   [correct]
- What would you do in that situation?   [correct]

If a verb other than "do" is used then it becomes possible to use "how" in the question, because you are asking "how" to do a specific action. For example:

- How can/should I prepare for the exam?   [correct]
- How would you react in that situation?   [correct]

5 Grammar Focus: Suggest and Recommend

Be careful about how you use the verbs 'suggest' and 'recommend'. Learners of English often use them incorrectly. Here are some common mistakes.

- ✗ I recommend/suggest you to see that movie.
- ✗ My friend recommended/suggested me that restaurant.

These verbs are normally followed by a noun, a gerund, or a that-clause.

NOUN
- I recommend/suggest the movie to you.
- My friend recommended/suggested the restaurant to me.

GERUND
- I recommend/suggest seeing the movie.
- My friend recommended/suggested trying the restaurant.

THAT-CLAUSE
- I recommend/ suggest (that) you (should) see the movie.
- My friend recommended/ suggested (that) I (should) try the restaurant.

Notice that in the that-clauses that are used with these verbs, both 'that' and the modal verbs can be left out. This causes some confusion for learners, so be careful.

6 Grammar: This Movie Is Dull. I Am Boring.

Keep in mind that adjectives for feelings and reactions often have two different forms, one ending in "-ed" and another ending in "-ing", "-y", "-ive", or "-ful". If you become confused and mistakenly use similar but incorrect adjective forms, the result can be amusing to your listeners.

For example, "I was <u>scary</u> at the zoo; I don't like animals." is grammatically correct but has a peculiar meaning. It means that other people at the zoo were frightened when they saw me. A much more common form would be "I was <u>scared</u> at the zoo."

You must also remember that the "-ed" form of some feelings/reactions adjectives can only be used if the subject is a person or a group of people. Therefore, a phrase such as "That topic is <u>embarrassed</u>" would be impossible because a "topic" does not have feelings and so cannot become "embarrassed". More acceptable phrases would be "That subject is <u>embarrassing</u>" or "I feel <u>embarrassed</u> talking about the subject".

7 Grammar: Conditionals

Conditional sentences link two actions, events, or situations, and express the idea that one follows from or depends on the other. They can be used to describe situations that are actual, possible, or imaginary. We will focus on Real Conditionals, which can be used to describe actual or possible situations.

Real Conditionals are used to describe the likely results of an action, event, or situation that is actual (in the past or present) or possible (in the future). They are formed of a dependent clause (if-clause) and an independent clause (main clause).

Zero Conditional for Present

If we want to say that one action, event, or situation usually or always follows from another, we can use the Present Real Conditional form (also called the Zero Conditional). It is formed as follows.

If-clause (present tense) + Main clause (present tense)

- If you heat water to 100 degrees Celsius, it boils.
- If I go out drinking until 3 in the morning, I can't go to work the next day.

Both 'if' and 'when' are used with Real Conditionals. Using 'if' suggests that something happens less frequently or occasionally. Using 'when' suggests that something happens regularly.

- When I have a day off, I usually go hiking. (I usually get a day off.)
- If I have a day off, I usually go hiking. (I infrequently get a day off.)

Type 1 Conditional for Future

Type 1 Conditionals (also known as Real Future Conditionals) are used to describe possible situations, events, or actions and their anticipated consequences. The form of Type 1 conditionals is as follows.

If-clause (present tense) + Main Clause (future tense)

If we don't work harder, we won't finish the project to meet the deadline.

We can also use 'if' and 'when' with Type 1 Conditionals. In this case, 'if' suggests that something is only a possibility, whereas 'when' suggest that something is inevitable.

- If you pay back the money you owe me, I'll lend you some more. (Maybe you won't.)
- When you pay back the money you owe me, I'll lend you some more. (I know you will eventually.)

We can also use different modals in the main clause to change the meaning.

- If he doesn't like it, he can leave.
- If he doesn't like it, he should leave.
- If he doesn't like it, he might leave.

Some expressions used with conditionals

Whenever / anytime	All A → B
Whenever I did something wrong, my parents spanked me.	
Only if	Only A → B
My parents spanked me only if I did something really bad.	
Unless	If not A → not B
My parents didn't spank me, unless I had done something terrible.	
Whether or not	A or not A → B
Whether or not they were angry with me, my parents always loved me.	
Even if / even when/ even though	A → B is expected but in this case, A –> not B
Even though I sometimes made my father mad, he never yelled at me.	
If / provided (that) / on the condition (that) / so long as / as long as	A → B
I got my allowance as long as I cleaned up my room.	

8 Usage: You "the Man"

Saying "I like the man who doesn't smoke" is okay if you are referring to a <u>specific group</u> of people (e.g.,"the five people sitting at the back of the room") and one of them doesn't smoke. However, if you are talking about <u>all</u> <u>people</u> or <u>all</u> <u>men</u> "the man who doesn't smoke" means the only man in the world who doesn't smoke. Since such a person doesn't exist, you might be wrong in talking about him. You probably mean to say "I like men who don't smoke."

Similarly, if you said "I like the guy in the black hat" and you were talking about all guys everywhere, then you would be wrong - but you would be CORRECT if you were talking about the one man wearing a black hat in a group of people.

9 Grammar: Have You Ever Been Experienced?

You will never hear a native English speaker ask, "Have you ever had an experience to do that?" or answer, "Yes, I have had an experience to do that" or "No, I have never had an experience to do that." That's because "have/had an experience to do" can always be replaced by the Present Perfect tense. A native speaker would simply say, "Have you ever done that?" and answer, "Yes, I have (done that)" or "No, I haven't (done that)." If you ever feel tempted to say, "...had an experience to [verb]" you should probably use a Present Perfect verb instead.

10 Usage: Breaking Up Is Hard To Do

If you are talking about the end of a romantic relationship, avoid using terms such as "We were <u>broken</u>" [wrong] or "I <u>was broken with</u> my boy/girlfriend" [wrong]. These terms make it sound like you were physically or emotionally broken but DO NOT give the listener any information about a romantic relationship. It would be correct to say, "We broke up" or "I broke up with my boy/girlfriend".

Also the phrases "I don't think of him as a man" and "I don't think of her as a woman" sound a little bit insulting in English ("He's not a real man; he's just a little baby!") and aren't used to describe someone's lack of romantic feelings towards another. Instead, a native speaker would say something like:

- I don't have any romantic feelings for him/her.
- I don't think of him/her as a possible boy/girlfriend.

11 Grammar: Real and Unreal Conditionals

When we say that some conditional sentences are 'unreal', we mean that they express situations that are impossible or at least highly unlikely.

- If I were a bird, I would lay an egg and make you an omelette.
  (However, I am not a bird.)
- If you hadn't been late, you wouldn't have gotten in trouble.
  (But you were late.)
- If I had time this weekend, I'd take you out for a nice dinner.
  (But, unfortunately, I won't have any time.)

Real versus Unreal Conditionals

Real Conditionals describe the likely result of an action, event or situation that is actual (in the past or present) or possible (in the future).

Unreal Conditionals describe the imagined result of an action, event or situation that is impossible or at least highly unlikely, so we talk about it hypothetically (as something imaginary).

Compare the meaning of the following.

▷ **Real Future**
- If I have time, I will take you out for dinner. (I might have time.)

 Unreal Future
- If I had time, I would take you out for dinner. (I won't have time.)

▷ **Real Present**
- If someone hits you, what do you do? (This sometimes happens.)

 Unreal Present
- If someone hit you, what would you do? (It's unlikely, but imaginable.)

▷ **Real Past**
- When Min Jung won the race, I was so happy for her. (She did win.)

 Unreal Past
- If Min Jung had won the race, I would've been so happy for her. (She didn't.)

12 Grammar: Past, Present, and Future Unreal Conditionals

Type 2 for Present and Future Unreal Conditionals

To talk about the Present or Future actions, events or situations that are impossible or highly unlikely and their imagined results, the Type 2 conditional. It is formed of a dependent (if-clause) and an independent (main) clause, as follows.

If-clause (past tense*) + Main clause (modal* + base form of verb).

- If I <u>had</u> any money, I <u>would</u> <u>lend</u> you some. (Present)
- If it <u>weren't</u> going to rain tomorrow, we <u>could</u> <u>go</u> surfing. (Future)

* It is just as common for the independent clause to come first. Notice that in this case, no comma is needed.
- I would lend you some money if I had some.
- We could go surfing if it weren't going to rain tomorrow.

* Notice that when using the verb 'to be' in the if-clause of an Unreal conditional, the form 'was' is not considered to be correct in formal English. In test situations, you should remember to always use 'were'. In informal English, however, 'was' is often used.
- If the product were priced more competitively, it might sell better.
- We could buy that car if it was a bit cheaper. (Informal)

* Since Unreal Conditionals are used only to refer to impossible or unlikely situations, the modals 'can', 'may' and 'shall' are not used with them because they are used to indicate possibilities. Instead, use 'could', 'might', and 'should'.

Past Unreal Conditionals are used to talk about imaginary actions, events, or situations in the past and their imagined consequences in the past. They are most commonly used to describe how the outcome might have been different if something in the past had occurred differently. Past Unreal Conditionals are also known as Type 3 Conditionals, and take the following form:

If-clause (past perfect tense) + Main clause (modal* + present perfect tense).
had + p.p.   have + p.p.

- Mr. Finch didn't pay me on time, so I quit working for him.
  If Mr. Finch had paid me on time, I wouldn't have quit working for him.

- I didn't have my camera with me, so I couldn't take a picture of the moose.
  If I had had my camera with me, I could have taken a picture of the moose.

13 Usage - What's Mine is Mine

Be careful about how you use possessives (ex. "my", "our", "Tony's", etc.). Many students have a tendency to use them in situations where they are unnecessary or just plain wrong. Take, for example, the phrases "I'm looking for my job" and "I will buy my car". In the first case, if you have not been given a job yet then it is not "your" job, so the phrase should be "I'm looking for a job". A similar thing is true of the second phrase; if you have not bought the car yet, it is not "your" car, so you should say, "I will buy a car".

It is also important to be cautious about using the verb "have" and possessives together. There is a critical difference between the way native English speakers use the phrases "I have a car" and "I have my car". "I have a car" means that I own a car although I <u>might</u> not have it here with me now. "I have my car," means that my car is here now (for example, "Don't worry if your car doesn't start; I have my car.").

14 Usage: Drunken Drunk

Koreans often misuse the word 'drunken'. Koreans say, "I am drunken," when native speakers of English would say, "I am drunk." As an adjective, the word 'drunken' is generally only used in front of a noun to describe the effects of excessive alcohol. For example, "There was a drunken party next door." "There is a drunken brawl on the street." "What shall we do with a drunken sailor?" But when the adjective follows the noun it modifies, we normally use 'drunk' rather than 'drunken'. For example, "She is drunk." "She got drunk." "I got drunk last night." "Let's get drunk tonight!" One exception to the above rule, however, is the expression 'drunk driving'.

Toasting each other is common in Western culture. Toasts such as "Here's to your health", "Bottoms up", "Down the hatch" or "Cheers" are used. "One shot" is Konglish.

It sounds strange to ask, "What is your drinking habit?" This is because to say that 'someone has a drinking habit' implies that you have reason to believe that he or she drinks too much alcohol. The terms 'drug habit' and 'gambling habit' have similar connotations.

If you want to know the amount of alcohol someone is able to comfortably drink, DO NOT ask them, "Can you drink well?" or "Are you strong to drink?" Instead, ask:

- Can you drink a lot?
- How much can you drink?

15 Usage: I played with my friends last night.

What do you think? Is this a correct sentence?

Actually, the sentence can be correct or incorrect, depending on who says it. If someone older than twelve said it, it would be wrong because the verb "play" seems too childish and is improper for an adult. Of course, it would be perfectly okay if a child said it.

Although it is okay for adults to "play" sports ("I played hockey yesterday"), "play" games ("We played poker"), "play" instruments ("She plays the piano"), and "play with" children or animals - adults DO NOT "play" by themselves or with their friends. Instead of "play", an adult would probably specify what sort of activity was going on (I went to a movie..., I went out drinking..., etc.) To speak more generally, you could use one of the following expressions.

	hung around	
I	**hung out**	with my friends last night.
	spent some time	

16 Usage: No "Skinship" Please

If you used the term "skinship" when talking with anyone who is not a fluent Konglish speaker, they would probably think you were talking about some strange boat made out of skin - in other words, they wouldn't understand you at all. The terms 'touching' or 'physical contact' are much better.

- × <u>Skinship</u> is very important for all people. [wrong]
- Touching is very important for all people. [correct]
- Physical contact is very important for all people. [correct]

Below is a list of some terms we use to describe different forms of physical contact between people:

- He has his arm around her shoulder.
- He has his arm around her waist.
- They are hand-in-hand.
- They are arm-in-arm.

17 Usage1: What a Rip Off!

"A rip off" (noun) is something that is highly over-priced.
- A hundred dollars for a plain white T-shirt?! What a rip-off!

Similarly, "to rip someone off" can mean to charge someone too much for something.
- If they are charging a hundred dollars, they are ripping people off.

"To be ripped off (by someone)" is the passive form of the same verb.
- People only shop here if they want to be ripped off!

"To rip off something" or "to rip something off" can also be used as verbs to mean 'steal' or 'remove'.
- Stephanie is really upset. Someone ripped off her car!
- He accidentally ripped the sleeve off his shirt.

"Rip-off" is even used as a noun to mean that an idea, piece of music, work of literature, or art has been 'stolen'.
- That song is a complete rip-off of the Osmonds' "Double Lovin'."

Usage2: Lend or Borrow?

Why is the question "Could you borrow me twenty dollars?" incorrect?

Be careful when using the verbs 'borrow' and 'lend'. 'Borrowing' describes <u>receiving</u> money on loan from someone. 'Lending' means <u>giving</u> someone money on loan. These verbs are often used incorrectly. Look at the following examples.
- A → $ → B   A **lends** $ to B.   Could you lend me twenty dollars?
- B ← $ ← A   B **borrows** $ from A.   Could I **borrow** twenty dollars from you?

18 Usage: Say, Tell, Talk, Speak

The verbs that are most commonly used with the reporting of speech are 'say' and 'tell'. Use 'say' when there is no need to mention the person(s) to whom something was said. 'Say' can refer to any kind of speech, but not usually with questions.
- He said he was tired.

Always use 'tell' when it is necessary to refer to the person(s) to whom something was said. 'Tell' is only used to mean 'inform' or 'instruct'.
- He told me he was tired.

When reporting speech, students of English commonly use the verbs 'talk' and 'speak' incorrectly. 'Talk' and 'speak' both refer to the act of speaking, and if we want to specify the topic, we must use the preposition 'about'. 'Talk' and 'speak' mean essentially the same thing, although 'speak' is usually used to refer to formal one-way speech (like lectures or sermons, etc.), or the use of a language.
- She spoke to us about Copernicus and Galileo.
- We talked about how we were going to invest the money.
- Did you know she speaks Swahili, Dutch, and English?

19 Grammar: Changes in Reported Speech

(1) Tense usually shifts one tense back in time

Although there are exceptions, the tense of the verb used in direct speech usually shifts one tense back in time when used in reported speech. (See chart in appendix for details.)

- She said, "I am tired." → She said (that) she was tired.
- Henry said, "I didn't do it!" → Henry told them (that) he hadn't done it.

(2) Time and place references change if necessary

If the time and place at which speech is reported are not the same as those at which something was originally said, any references to time and place must be changed accordingly.
Soo Jung said, "I ran into my friend here yesterday." → Soo Jung told us that she had run into her friend there the day before.

(3) Personal pronouns change if necessary

In general, personal pronouns change to the third person singular ('he/she') or plural ('they'), except when the speaker is reporting his or her own words.
Rita said, "I met Jean on the first day of school." → Rita said that she had met Jean on the first day of school.

20 Grammar: The Long and the Short of It

Students sometimes make mistakes like the following:
✗ I slept at one a.m. last night.

This doesn't sound correct, and it isn't. No native speaker would use the verb 'slept' in this context. 'Slept' is used to describe an action that normally occurs over a relatively long duration of time, as in the following examples.

- I slept for seven hours last night.
- I slept until noon.

The problem with the incorrect sentence above is that the action being described happens at one moment ('at one a.m. last night'), not over a longer period of time. To express the intended meaning, you'd need to use a different verb, such as 'to fall asleep' or 'go to bed', as in:

- I fell asleep at 1 a.m. last night.
- I went to bed at 1 a.m. last night.

There are many other examples of this confusion between verbs that describe actions occurring at one moment and those describing actions occurring over longer periods of time.

'to wake up' or 'to awaken' versus 'to stay awake' or 'to stay up'

- I woke up at 8 o'clock this morning.
- I stayed awake all night.

'to put on something' or 'to get dressed' versus 'to wear'

- I got dressed as fast as I could.
- I wore the same clothes I was wearing the day before.

SLE 3A Textbook Recordings

Track	Title
1	Introduction
2	Lesson 1 - Reading
3	Lesson 1 - Dialogue
4	Lesson 2 - Reading
5	Lesson 3 - Dialogue
6	Lesson 3 - Reading
7	Lesson 4 - Reading
8	Lesson 5 - Dialogue
9	Lesson 6 - Dialogue
10	Lesson 7 - Dialogue
11	Lesson 8 - Dialogue
12	Lesson 9 - Dialogue
13	Lesson 10 - Dialogue
14	Lesson 11 - Dialogue
15	Lesson 11 - Reading
16	Lesson 12 - Dialogue
17	Lesson 13 - Dialogue
18	Lesson 14 - Dialogue
19	Lesson 15 - Dialogue
20	Lesson 16 - Dialogue
21	Lesson 16 - Reading
22	Lesson 17 - Dialogue
23	Lesson 17 - Activity B
24	Lesson 19 - Dialogue
25	Lesson 19 - Reading
26	Lesson 20 - Reading